Business Letter Writing

BUSINESS LETTER WRITER

Jenny and Tim Saville

WARD LOCK

© Jenny and Tim Saville 1981

First published in Great Britain in 1981
by Ward Lock Limited, Villiers House, 41–47 Strand,
London WC2N 5JE, a Cassell company.

Reprinted 1986, 1987, 1988, 1989 (twice), 1990

Designed by Charlotte Westbrook

House editor Suzanna Osman-Jones

Text set in Century Schoolbook

Printed and bound in Great Britain by
William Collins, Glasgow

British Library Cataloguing in Publication Data

Saville, Jenny
  Business letter writer.
  1. Communication in management
  I. Title   II. Saville, Tim
  651.7′4   HF5718

  ISBN 0-7063-6491-0

Contents

Chapter sections and model letters

1 Introduction 12

2 Letters in connection with employment 36

3 General business letters 69

4 Accounts department correspondence   88

1 Introduction

Your correspondence will conjure up a picture of you, or you together with your organization in the mind of the person receiving it. Letter-writing is one of the main ways in which you can establish a business relationship with the world at large; and a well-written, well-displayed letter will create more good-will or win more customers for your company than a poor letter will.

Whoever you write to, we hope this book will help you write the sort of letter that gives the impression that yours is an efficient though friendly organization; and that you as an individual are pleasant and direct to deal with.

As well as including chapters on writing technique and things to avoid when writing letters, the book includes a selection of business letters for many occasions. The letters, of course, are not meant to be copied word for word. You need not be afraid to let your personality show through in your letters and you can make modifications to the model letters to give your correspondence a personal touch.

It goes without saying that all the names, addresses and letters throughout the book are completely imaginary.

First things first, a letter-writer's checklist

When you compose your letter, consider these points:

1   What am I writing about? Do I have all the

necessary information? In which order should I present it?

2 Who am I writing to, what are their needs?

3 How much do they know about the subject of my letter?

4 What am I trying to achieve?

5 What obstacles in my reader's mind must I overcome – cost, prejudice, boredom?

6 Why should the person I am writing to want my product or service? How can I seize his or her attention? What will interest him or her?

7 Where and when will my letter be read?

8 Am I using short words, short sentences and short paragraphs? They will make the letter easier to read and understand. 'Overwrite' and then cut your letter – never 'underwrite' and expand it.

9 Am I considering spelling, grammar and punctuation?

10 Have I finished my letter by asking for action? The real job of a business letter-writer is usually to persuade his or her reader to act.

A business letter may be hand-written or typed, but always make it as neat and legible as possible. Use black or blue ink, not colours. It is wise to keep a copy for future reference; a carbon copy if it is typed or written with a ballpoint pen, or a photocopy, or you can make notes of what you have said.

If you have access to a typewriter or a typist so much the better. Whether typed or not, lay out your letter on the correct size of paper, make it look attractive. Margins are important, they stop the letter looking like a dull mass of type, much too daunting to read. Capitals, indented paragraphs, underlined headings and numbered points can make your letters clearer – though numbered points *can* look a trifle official.

What to avoid when writing

Avoid commercialese or commercial English

Avoid commercialese, it will make your letters seem pompous, old-fashioned and off-hand. If you would not use a phrase when speaking to someone face-to-face, do not use it in a letter. Commercialese won't make your letter more official or legal, just starchy and confusing.

Do not use:	*Instead, perhaps use:*
Letter openings	
We acknowledge receipt of your letter	Thank you for your letter
We are in receipt of your favour	Many thanks for your letter
We beg to acknowledge receipt of your letter	We have received your letter
Adverting to your favour	With reference to your letter
Re your letter	Referring to your letter
Yours to hand	We are writing to inform you
We beg to inform you	We are writing to let you know
Letter endings	
Awaiting the favour of your reply	I hope to hear from you soon
The favour of your early reply will oblige	
Assuring you of our best attention	Omit
Trusting we may be favoured by the receipt	

14

Other expressions

Enclosed herewith	I am enclosing
Attached please find	I enclose
Enclosed please find	I attach
	Here is
Trusting our action meets with your approval	Do you agree? What do you think of this suggestion?
We beg to remain	omit
same	Your letter, the order, the goods, etc.
ult, inst, prox	*give each month its name*
viz	namely
under separate cover	separately *or better still state how:* by parcel post, by airmail, etc.
hereto	omit
even/current date	*give the date*

Avoid extravagant language

Write simply and naturally, using the simple word rather than the elaborate one.

Do not use:	Instead, perhaps use:
accomplish	do
acquaint	tell
acquire	get, gain
approximately	about
ascertain	find out
assist	help
commence	start, begin
communicate	tell, write
communication	letter, postcard
considerable	large

currently	now
description	sort
desire	wish
despatch	send
discover	find
donate	give
endeavour	try
expeditious	prompt
facilitate	make easier
forward	send
implement	carry out
inform	tell
initiate	begin
involve	include
majority (of)	most
materialize	take place
note	see
obtain	get
ongoing	continuing
peruse	read
practically	almost
prevent	stop
purchase	buy
remit	pay or send
remuneration	pay, wages, salary
regret (we)	are sorry
render	give
request	ask
state	tell, say, mention
solicit custom	invite custom
terminate	end
trust	hope
utilize	use

When to avoid technical expressions

There is nothing wrong with using the specialist terms of a subject if you are sure all your readers will understand them, but it is not fair to your correspondents to use technical terminology simply to make your subject seem more mysterious to an outsider. Unless you are sure your correspondent understands the specialist terms of your business, try to get your message across in general everyday language. Never use a technical term just because it *looks* technical.

Another danger of using technical language is that some words mean one thing in everyday speech and another in their technical context. Make sure you will not confuse your correspondent.

Avoid circumlocution!

To use a longer phrase than is necessary is only justified when it will help your reader to understand the meaning.

Do not use:	Instead, perhaps use:
in the event that	if
with regard to	
concerning	about
respecting	
in respect of	
it is my opinion that	I think, I believe
in order to	to
with a view to	
prior to	before
in the amount of	for
shall take steps to	shall
consequent upon	after
due to the fact that	because, as

17

in the course of	during
at this point in time, at this moment	now
come to a decision	decide

Avoid tautology

Tautology means repetition of the same phrase or word or idea in different words, for example; They fell down one after the other *in succession;* the *true* facts; *close* proximity.

Avoid words whose meaning you do not know

Use a dictionary, never guess at the meaning of a word. Make sure you do not confuse words like disinterested/uninterested, comprise/compose, practical/practicable, imply/infer, prescribe/proscribe, stationery/stationary, compliment/complement, affect/effect, principal/principle.

If you find it difficult to differentiate between pairs of words, you might find it useful to invent a sentence or rhyme to help you remember which word to use, for example 'e' for 'envelope' will show you that 'stationery' is the right word; and if you remember that 'principal' has an 'a' for 'authority' in it, you will never get principal/principle confused.

Avoid foreign phrases

Foreign phrases, especially Latin tags, are out of place in everyday business correspondence. Apart from well-established expressions like *per cent,* use an English equivalent.

Avoid slang

While slang is acceptable in everyday speech it should not be used in business letters.

Avoid clichés

Beware of using clichés; they will make your letters and reports appear hackneyed. If there is a better way of expressing what you want to say, use it. Phrases to avoid include 'be that as it may', 'fact of the matter', 'in the not too distant future', 'to all intents and purposes'.

Avoid overworked abstractions

Instead of saying 'on a monthly basis', use 'monthly'. Do not say you 'are not in a position' to do something, let your correspondent know you 'cannot'. Do not talk about 'canteen facilities', when you mean 'canteen'.

Do not refer to a 'redundancy situation' when you mean 'redundancy'. Abstract words are not only vague, they lead to longer, more roundabout sentences. Stop and think again before you use words like preparation, nature, position, event, situation, sphere, matter, steps, view, degree, condition, application. Turn your sentence round! Be direct and brief.

Style and grammar

Apart from commercialese, there are other forms of style which can make letters seem very pompous, and which you should avoid. For example, people too often use the *passive* voice rather than the *active* voice which causes their letters to be impersonal and often difficult to understand. They put 'your amendments have been noted' rather than 'I note your amendments', 'the application form was not sent with your letter' rather than 'you did not send the application form with your letter'. Here is a particularly bad example which is bordering on the ludicrous: 'investigations have been begun to be made', when the writer could have said 'we have begun to investigate'.

It all comes back to a simple but fundamental rule – write to people in much the same way as you would talk to them. Surely you would never say to someone 'Your letter has been received and our accounts department will be asked to render the account'. You would say – and should write – 'Thank you for your letter. I have asked our accounts department to send you the account'. Try to use the active voice rather than the passive voice as much as possible.

If you put adverbs in the wrong part of a sentence, you can cause ambiguity and change the meaning of the sentence. For example:
'we gave you credit of *only* £1,000' (meaning, we gave you £1,000 credit and no higher);
'*only* we gave you credit of £1,000' (meaning, we and nobody else, gave you £1,000 credit).

To write well, you must use good grammar, without being pedantic about it. Much grammar is common-sense, such as putting a phrase in the right part of a sentence. For example, if you write '*As a long-standing customer*, I am surprised that you have not settled your account promptly', you would be wrongly suggesting that you, the writer, were the long-standing customer. You should put 'I am surprised that you, *as a long-standing customer*, have not settled our account promptly.'

Adjectives and adverbs can help your reader to picture ideas but they can complicate things if you use too many of them, as for example; 'The newly introduced, particularly recommended, extra-speedy Royal Mail Special Delivery Service'.

Do not make your sentences too long or complicated nor introduce too many topics or ideas in a single sentence. Your average sentence should be around sixteen to twenty words in length – though you should try to vary the lengths of your sentences.

Punctuation

The purpose of punctuation is to break up the text into understandable sections and make the writer's meaning clear.

The table below shows the various punctuation marks and explains how to use them and how to type them.

Punctuation mark	Examples of use	How to type
full stop .	End of a sentence (full stops are also used to denote abbreviations).	Leave two spaces after a typewritten full stop before beginning the next sentence.
comma ,	Marks a pause in a sentence. Marks off items in a list or series. Separates the main clauses in a sentence. Marks off a parenthesis. The use or non-use of a comma can sometimes change the meaning of a sentence. Use commas with care.	No space before a comma; one space after.

colon :	Introduces a list of items, a quotation or an explanation. Marks and separates two equal balanced statements.	No space before a colon; one space after.
semi-colon ;	Separates clauses in a sentence.	No space before a semi-colon; one space after.
dash —	Can be used to add another idea to the end of a sentence. An alternative to parentheses (brackets) – it marks off an aside or an interruption.	One space before a dash and one space after.
hyphen -	Used to form compound nouns and compound adjectives. Used after certain prefixes, particularly where two vowels must be pronounced separately. Used for word division at the end of a line.	No space before or after a hyphen.
Brackets () or sometimes [] (also called parentheses)	Must be used in pairs. Mark off an interruption or aside. As a safeguard against mistakes, sums of money expressed in figures are often repeated in words, typed inside round brackets. Square brackets are far less common	If you need to type a square bracket, and there is not one on your typewriter, you should use the oblique sign, / (solidus) with the underscore. For the opening bracket, type the oblique sign (solidus) sign, /, backspace once

than round brackets and are very rarely used in letter-writing.

and type the underscore. Next turn the platen (roller on which the paper rests) back one line space and type the underscore, then turn the platen forward a single line space, back-space once and then continue your typing until you need to type the closing bracket. Again, type the oblique (solidus) sign. Now back-space twice and type the under-score. Turn the platen back one line space and type the underscore. Finally turn the platen forward a single line space, leave one space and then continue typing.

inverted commas or quotation marks (single) ' '
or sometimes (double) " "

Always used in pairs. Used when reporting direct speech – rare in business corres-pondence. Also used to mark the names of books, plays etc. and when words or phrases are used in a special sense.

No space before; one space after. Whether to use single or double quotation marks is a matter of personal preference, though you should be consistent. Single quotation marks are more usual. If you need to show a quotation within another quotation you should use one style of quotation mark for the main quotation and the other for the secondary quotation, for example: *He said, 'Is the "Bunch of Grapes" down this road?'*

omission marks ...	Used with a direct quotation which has been shortened, for example: *'... a really excellent book... splendid photographs'*.	Three full stops.
exclamation mark !	The exclamation mark is used at the end of a sentence to indicate surprise, excitement or with an order such as *Attention!* It is very rarely used in business correspondence.	If the character is not provided on your typewriter, the exclamation mark can be produced by typing the apostrophe and then backspacing and typing a full stop below it. Leave no space before an exclamation mark, two spaces after it before beginning the next sentence.
question mark ?	The question mark is used at the end of a sentence after a direct question, where the writer is using the same words he might use if speaking to his correspondent. However, the	When typing leave no space before the question mark, two spaces after it, before the beginning the next sentence.

24

question mark is not needed in polite requests made in the form of questions, which are often used in business corres- pondence, for example *Would you please let me know when we may expect delivery.*

Layout

The letters in this book are laid out in the various styles used in most business letters. The most common ways of displaying a letter are the indented paragraph (see the letter on page 38) and the blocked paragraph (see page 36). In long letters, particularly those which deal with several different topics, you may choose to use the headed paragraph (see page 53), numbering each paragraph or giving it a heading, or both.

Some organizations prescribe the layout to be used in all their business correspondence. Even if you are allowed a free choice of how to set out your letters you will probably find it best to adopt either the indented or blocked paragraph style and use it all the time.

Whichever style you use, present your letters in a professional way on good quality paper. If you have the address printed, use a good printer. Headed paper, continuation paper and envelopes should match each other. It is well worth spending some time in choosing a style of letter-head which creates the right impression of your firm. A flowing script will suggest that yours is an old-established (though hopefully not old-fashioned) company, whereas a *sans serif* typeface will give a very modern impression.

A qualified designer will be able to design a range of stationery for your company that will reflect the image you are trying to create. Your letter-head should indicate the type of business you run, unless this is clear from the name of your company. The letter-head should not only include the address and telephone number but the telegraphic address as well and Telex number if you have one. With certain exceptions, letter-heads must show the name of all the directors and partners. Where a director of a registered company is not British, his or her nationality must also be shown. Registered companies must also display the registered number, place of registration and the address of the registered office, unless they have received exemption from this.

Whether the indented or blocked style is used, the business letter will consist of these parts:

1 **Your address** (which is probably in the printed letter heading). Show your postcode, telephone number and Telex and Fax numbers.

2 **The date.** In Britain the method of expressing the date is that the day is followed by the month and then the year. The date is usually written with ordinal numbers: 25th May 1979. However dates written 28 October 1948 are equally acceptable. Do not use the shortened forms, 14.10.1900 or 11.8.80, as these are confusing, particularly in correspondence with the United States, where it is usual to write the date in the order of month, day, year. It is also a bad idea to use 'Date as Postmark', as in most organizations the envelope is thrown away when the letter is opened.

3 **The reference.** Rather than giving a reference within the body of the letter, quote your reference and your correspondent's reference at the top of the letter. Many printed letter headings provide for the reference by incorporating a space in which they can be inserted or the design may include Your ref: followed by a space, and Our ref: with a space.

A reference often consists of the initials of the person dictating the letter and of the typist, for example, JSM/fgs, or MB/SR. Other references may identify a department, or be linked to a filing system.

The specimen letters show various types of reference. The reference is normally typed under

27

the firm's printed letter-heading at the left-hand margin. Occasionally it is typed in the bottom left-hand corner of he paper.

4 **The addressee.** The name and address of the person or organization you are writing to will appear on the top left hand side of the paper, usually three single line spaces after the reference or date. The inside address is always typed in block form. It should be exactly the same as that on the envelope. Mr or Esq, Mrs, Miss or Ms and Messrs or Mmes are the most common courtesy titles used to address correspondents. Though these are all abbreviations they may be written with or without a full stop after them. This is a matter of personal preference, or may be laid down in a firm's house style; it is more contemporary to omit the full stop. You can simply put the person's first name and surname, but it is more polite to use a courtesy title if you do not know them well.

The use of Esq (Esquire) sometimes causes confusion. Originally it was a title used for a man of gentle birth who attended a knight, but nowadays some firms use it when writing to all gentlemen. Other firms use Mr in all cases. As Esq and Mr are alternative forms it is of course wrong to use them both together; for example, Mr Arthur Crease Esq is incorrect.

A married woman is often addressed by her husband's initials or name and not her own, so that Lucy Jones, the wife of Martin Jones, may be addressed as Mrs Martin Jones, or Mrs M. Jones. Many women, however, prefer to be addressed by their own first names. In addition widows and divorced women use their own initials or first name, and this form is increasing in popularity for all women, e.g. Mrs Lucy Jones.

Where two ladies have the same name, such as a mother-in-law and her daughter-in-law, who may both be Mrs Brian Hughes, the younger may be addressed Mrs Brian Hughes, Jun., or Jnr., but it is incorrect to write to the older as Mrs Brian Hughes, Sen.

Ms may be used if it is the woman's personal preference or if you do not know whether the woman you are writing to is single or married. In such cases you may also use Miss. If you are writing to a married woman who has continued to use her maiden name, you should address her as Ms or Miss. Single women are of course addressed as Miss or Ms and two unmarried sisters as The Misses Mary and Louise Lane.

Where a person holds a title such as Doctor, Colonel, Dame, they should be addressed by that title, which replaces the use of Mr, Mrs, Miss, Ms and Esq. Doctor is abbreviated e.g. Dr Smith.

When a person is entitled to letters after their name it is usual to include them. The letters denote honours, decorations, university degrees, membership of professional or learned societies. When letters are included it is important to list them in order of their status.

(a) Orders of Chivalry: There are nine Orders of Chivalry in Britain. If a person has received several all the letters must be included after his name. They must be listed starting with the highest. A higher grade of a junior Order precedes a lower grade of a more senior Order, e.g. Sir John Smith, GBE, KCMG, CB, CVO.

(b) Decorations: start with the highest, e.g. John Smith Esq, MC, QGM.

(c) Crown Appointments.

29

(d) University degrees: start with the lowest. Honorary doctorates conferred on royalty or other people who are distinguished in other walks of life than the academic should not be used in correspondence.

(e) Professional qualifications: these are not used in social correspondence but only if you are writing to someone in connection with his or her profession, e.g. when writing to an architect you write Mr John Smith, A.R.I.B.A.

(f) Letters denoting a profession, e.g. Captain John Smith, RN. (All naval officers below Rear-Admiral rank are entitled to have RN after their name even if retired).

A general rule to remember is that the more lasting an honour, the nearer its initials should be placed to the holder's name. Letters after the name are always expressed in capitals, and it is a matter of preference whether or not you put a full stop after each letter. When a person holds a number of decorations it is sufficient to use just one or two of the highest ranking ones.

Messrs. This shortening of Messieurs is becoming rather old-fashioned. It may be used when writing to a partnership, e.g. Messrs. Smythe and Hythe, where the firm's name includes the name of the partners, or a partner. However, it cannot be used if the personal name begins with *The* e.g. The Smythe Engineering Co., or where the personal name already has a title, e.g. Sir Andrew Douglas & Co.

Of course it would be quite wrong to write 'Messrs Speedy Cleaners'. It is also incorrect to use Messrs when writing to an individual of a firm, e.g. you should write to 'Mr Mark Adams,

Braithwaite and Co.' Never use 'Messrs' when writing to a limited company or a chartered or statutory corporation.

5 **The salutation.** This consists of 'Dear . . .' plus the person's name or Sir, Sirs, Madame or Mesdames, or sometimes just 'Gentlemen' when writing to a company. Type the salutation three single line spaces below the inside address or the date. (See the examples on pages 36 and 37.) A person's name is his or her favourite word, so if you know the name, use it. Begin typing at the left hand margin and type the first letter of each word in capitals.

6 **Heading.** If you think it will help your reader, give your letter a heading. Make it simple, but complete enough to make the subject of the letter clear.

When a letter has a subject heading you should leave two single line spaces after the salutation; then type the heading, which in fully blocked letters should be started at the left hand margin, and then leave two single line spaces before typing the body of the letter. A heading is usually typed in upper and lower case and underlined.

No full stop should be typed after the last word unless this happens to be an abbreviation.

7 **Body of the letter.** As a general rule this should be typed in single line spacing with double line spacing between each paragraph. A short letter may, however, be typed in double line spacing, using double line spacing between paragraphs.

If there has been previous correspondence, refer to it in the first paragraph. Avoid a formal opening. Get to the point quickly. Break up the letter into readable paragraphs, confining each paragraph to one idea or topic. Write simply and courteously. Keep the person you are writing to in mind. Sounds obvious? Yes, it is, but many people still write letters in technical terms to laymen, who may not understand. Avoid clichés and commercialese.

Use numbered points or headings only if they will be helpful to your reader: They make letters more formal. They do, however, make the various points stand out very clearly.

You might consider making certain important points in your letter stand out by displaying them so they catch your reader's eye; leave one line space above and below the facts you wish to emphasize. Sometimes information can usefully be displayed in columns within the body of a fully blocked letter.

The last paragraph shoud be positive. Avoid hackneyed phrases like 'Assuring you of our best attention at all times'. If you decide to start the final paragraph with a participle, be sure to add 'I am', or 'We are'. However, it is better to avoid starting with a participle altogether, and instead of writing 'Hoping to hear from you soon, I am', say, 'I hope to hear from you soon'. It is often a good idea to end with a question, e.g. 'Do you agree?'. Then your reader will know you are expecting a reply to your letter.

Leave two single-line spaces at the end of the letter, then type the complimentary close.

8 **Complimentary close.** This must match the salutation. If you have used 'Dear Sir (s)', 'Dear Madame' or 'Mesdames', you should close your letter with 'Yours faithfully'. You may also use 'Yours truly', which implies a rather more personal relationship. You may also come across

'Yours very truly', 'Yours respectfully' and even 'Your obedient servant', but these are rare in modern business correspondence.

If you have addressed your correspondent by name use 'Yours sincerely', or if you know them very well you can put 'Best wishes' first, or you may choose 'Yours ever'. 'Yours affectionately' should only be used between very close friends.

9 **The signature.** Even if your signature is easy to read, it is good practice to type the name of the person signing the letter and their job title, e.g.
Stephen Bevin
Housing Department.

A woman normally indicates whether she wishes to be addressed as Mrs, Miss or Ms, e.g. Mary Smith (Miss).

An official, for example a Company Secretary, may give, above his signature, the name of the company for which he is signing. When he writes in the plural 'we', he *must* do so.

A partner signing a letter for his firm writes the name of the firm, not his own name:

Pickthwaite, Borrie & Co.

Never sign your letters with a rubber stamp. If a letter is worth sending, surely it is worth signing personally.

10 **Enclosure.** List the reference numbers of any enclosures at the bottom of the letter, not in the text, e.g.
'Enclosures: Leaflets PD 147 and HB 283'.

Addressing envelopes

Use good quality envelopes with as little 'show through' as possible. It may be worth having your company's name and address printed in the top left hand corner of your envelopes so that if letters are undelivered for any reason they can be returned unopened.

Envelopes should match your company's letter head paper, both in style and size, so you will not have to fold your letters more than is necessary. Always use an envelope that is large enough and strong enough to take the letter and any enclosures.

The address should be typed on the lower half of the envelope, parallel to the length of the envelope rather than the breadth. Single line spacing and the block style are most suitable on a small envelope. If typing a larger envelope it may be best to indent each line of the address and to type it in double line spacing so it will be easier to read. Instructions such as 'Private', 'Personal', 'Confidential', should be typed in capital letters and underlined. Type them two lines above the addressee's name. The address should be typed at least 40mm (1½in) from the top of the envelope so it will be kept clear of the stamp or the impression made by the franking machine.

Type the name of the town in capital letters. It is not always necessary to include the name of the county but you should use the postcode if you know it – this will speed delivery. A postcode is a combination of up to seven letters and numbers which enables letters to be machine coded and then sorted electronically at each stage of their journey. The first part of the code refers to the Postcode Area. Each area is divided into smaller districts which are represented by the number in the first half of the postcode. Postcode districts are divided into smaller units called Sectors and then into very small areas which cover about fifteen addresses or may in fact only cover one organization if it receives a large quantity of mail.

The postcode should always be the last item in an address and ideally should have a line by itself. If there is no room to give the postcode a separate line, type it to the right of the last line of the address leaving a clear space in front of the postcode.

Letters from overseas should still include the postcode as the final item in the address, preferably on a separate line. Do not type or write anything below the postcode or to the right of the postcode. The postcode must be typed in capital letters. Do not use any punctuation between or after the characters in the postcode, nor underline it. One or two spaces should be left between the two halves of the postcode.

You should type the envelope for each letter as soon as you have typed the letter itself. Do not forget to include all enclosures. Some firms find it helpful to affix a brightly coloured sticker to letters which will have enclosures, otherwise you can list enclosures at the bottom of the letter.

When using long envelopes with flaps at the end the flap should be on the left side.

2 Letters in connection with employment

Letter excusing absence from work

15 Moye Avenue,
Penshurst, Kent
PH5 6WX
Tel: Penshurst (0521-13) 5821

15th April 19__

Mr P. Mahoney,
Conran Investments Ltd.,
Penshurst, Kent
PH9 3CG

Dear Mr Mahoney,

I confirm that I left a telephone message with your personal assistant this morning to explain that I was feeling too ill to come to work. I subsequently went to my GP who diagnosed an infection of the respiratory tract. I enclose the medical certificate from which you will see that I shall probably be off work at least ten days.

I have spoken to Arthur Crease about my work commitments for the next few days and I believe that things are under control, but if anybody has any problems about my work they should not hesitate to telephone me.

Yours sincerely,

Michael Young

Letter requesting leave of absence

> 8 Pinter Green,
> Pearson Cross,
> Surrey, GU8 5BV

T. Gerald Esq.,
Gerald and Kirkdale Ltd.,
5 Heath Approach,
Pearson Cross,
Surrey,
GU5 4ED

28th October 19__

Dear Mr Gerald,

I have just received a summons for Jury Service for the two weeks beginning 8th December. I should therefore be most grateful if you would give me leave of absence for that period.

> Yours sincerely,

> Susan Parker

Letter of application for salary increase

5 Lucknow Mansions
High Street
TOTNES
Devon TQ9 8FG

1st March 19___

J. Settle Esq
Hartley & Kenny Ltd
5 Hornbean Way
Totnes
Devon
TQ4 7UV

Dear Mr Settle,

You may not be aware that although I have been employed by the Company for eighteen months I have received no increase in my salary of £X a year.
You will of course appreciate that during this time there has been a very large increase in the cost of living and I have recently been finding it very difficult to manage. In addition, I have been given greater responsibility since the restructuring of the department last year.

I should therefore be grateful if you would consider my request favourably.

Yours sincerely

David J. Simpson

Letter thanking employer for salary increase

5 Lucknow Mansions
High Street
TOTNES
Devon TQ9 8FG

5th March 19__

J. Settle Esq
Hartley & Kenny Ltd
5 Hornbean Way
Totnes
Devon
TQ4 7UV

Dear Mr Settle,

I am very grateful to you for raising my salary by £X a year. I will do everything I can to justify the increase.

Yours sincerely

David J. Simpson

Letter asking for promotion

56 Northgate Rd.,
BOLTON, BL4 5HF

14th May 19__

C. C. Lauton Esq
5 Hyde Road
BOLTON
BL8 4RF

Dear Mr Lauton,

I understand that Mr Brand, the firm's chief buyer, is retiring next month and I would like to apply for his job.

As you know, I have been with the firm as a senior buyer for six years and have an additional fifteen years' experience as a buyer in other textile firms. I feel therefore that I have a comprehensive knowledge of all aspects of the trade which would enable me to act as chief buyer. You will remember that I deputized for Mr Brand for four months when he was on sick leave.

Yours sincerely,

A. P. Howard

Applying for a job

Replying to an advertisement

At the outset of a business career, or when you are looking for a better job, the letter of application is of paramount importance. It will be sent to an unknown reader and may have to compete with hundreds of other letters. The fact that your letter will be one among many should not put you off, but rather encourage you to plan and write your letter so it will stand out from the others.

Unless the advertisement to which you are replying specifically asks candidates to apply in handwriting, it creates a better impression if you type letters of application, especially if your handwriting is not as neat as it might be. Never send a printed or duplicated letter. It is certainly worth the extra effort of typing each letter individually. Write your letters with the particular post for which you are applying firmly in mind. Try and show you know something about the firm in question and the nature of their business. Select relevant experience from your career which could be useful in the job in question and describe this. A job advertisement usually sets out the qualities the employer is looking for and in replying to the advertisement you must show that you possess those qualities.

Use good quality, preferably plain, white paper of a standard business size. Write or type on one side of the paper only. Your letter should be brief and come to the point straightaway. If you have obtained written references from previous employers or others who know you well, you may wish to enclose copies of these testimonials. Never, however, enclose the originals, not only because they could get lost in the post but because you may need to send copies to a number of prospective employers.

It is probably best to mention that you have written references, press cuttings, certificates or specimens of your work, but not to send copies of them until you are asked to do so. Before putting your letter in its envelope check that there are no mistakes in it – don't forget that if your letter has errors in typing, spelling or grammar it will almost certainly be discarded immediately. Keep a copy of the letter so you can refer to it before the interview and so you can use it as a model for future letters.

Most employment agencies and many employers, particularly those who employ a large staff, ask job applicants to fill out an application form. Before filling out such a form it is a good idea to take a copy of it and complete that as a trial run. (Incidentally, if you ever have to design a form, try completing it before you have copies printed. Such forms are often badly designed, leaving candidates too little space to type in the information requested. Often many of the facts asked for are irrelevant in any case.)

Application forms usually ask for the candidate's date of birth, nationality, marital status, numbers and ages of children (information which is surely of no importance unless accommodation is provided with the post in question), training, giving dates, previous posts and present post giving dates, examinations passed, areas of the country in which the applicant would consider working, present salary or salary range, hobbies and other interests and the names and addresses of two referees. Candidates may also be invited to state on a separate sheet of paper the experience gained in their present and previous posts and to explain its relevance to the post now sought.

When completing such forms try to pick out areas of your experience which you feel will be useful to a prospective employer. Sound enthusiastic about your previous and present jobs. Do not give your reasons for

42

leaving previous jobs or for seeking a new job unless you are specifically asked to do so. The reasons you give – if you are obliged to give any – must be acceptable ones. For example, it is quite all right to say you are looking for more responsibility or more money but never say you are leaving because you have been passed over for promotion or that you are overworked.

If you are asked to state your present salary do not put a higher figure – you are bound to be found out. When listing hobbies and other interests be selective. Choose from your interests those which demonstrate some of the qualities needed in the job in question. This is particularly important for those looking for their first job as they cannot draw from their work experience. It may be best not to mention political, religious or trades union activities in case these prejudice a prospective employer.

Letter applying for an advertised job

9 Nelson Close
London NW3 7BT
5th January 19__

The Personnel Manager
Harley and Johnson
7 Norwood Parade
London
NW6 5RF

Dear Sir

Re: Advertisement for Director's Secretary
    The Times 4th January

I am replying to your advertisement in yesterday's Times and wish to apply for the post of Director's Secretary.

For the past three years I have been employed by Messrs Z & K Rossfield as a secretary to one of the Branch Managers. My duties have included confidential secretarial work, book-keeping and supervising the clerks in the post room. As well as having good shorthand speeds and being accustomed to audio typing, I am responsible for answering most of the routine correspondence myself.

Yours faithfully

M. Styles

School-leaver applying for a job

If you are a school or college leaver looking for your first job you will have no experience of the type of work for which you are applying but you should try and mention points from your school career or outside interests which show you have the qualities needed to do the job. For example, organizing a stall at the school fête and running it with a band of helpers could show the prospective employer you have a talent for getting things done, self reliance and ability to get on with other people. Hobbies, memberships of school societies or sports teams, voluntary work or holiday jobs can be mentioned to show that you have the qualities and initiative needed to do the job for which you are applying. It is particularly important to list examinations passed and relevant non-examination subjects which have been studied.

Letter from school-leaver applying for a job

Luton Cottage,
Barfield Road,
Esher, Surrey,
KT2 3RE

17th July 19___

The Shop Manager,
Linton Ltd.,
9 Suffolk Place,
Esher, Surrey,
KT3 4BL

Dear Sir,

In reply to your advertisement in this week's 'Esher Mercury' I would like to apply for the position of sales assistant. I have just left school after taking 'O' levels and am keen to make my career in retailing as I enjoy meeting people. During my school holidays I worked in two supermarkets and in a gift shop in Kingston and I also ran the school bookshop for two terms.

I enclose a copy of a testimonial from my Headmaster and would be glad to give you the names of two other people who have known me for some years and would testify to my character.

I could come for an interview at any time convenient to you.

Yours faithfully,

James Prout

Enclosure.

Enquiring about possible job vacancies

You can, of course, approach organizations which you feel may be able to use your skills, and enquire about possible vacancies. In this way you may be offered a job for which you will have no competitors as the vacancy may have arisen very recently and the job will not yet have been advertised. Such letters should be individually written to refer to the organization in question.

Whilst keeping your letter short, you must convey the impression that you have singled out this one organization because you feel they are the most prestigious in their field and you have always wanted to work for them. Address your letter to a named person wherever possible and find out as much as you can about the organization in question. Telephone them and ask the switchboard operator for the name of the personnel director or the head of the division or department you are applying to, so that you can write to him or her by name and at the same time ask for a copy of the organization's literature or sales catalogue to be sent to you.

Letter enquiring about possible job vacancies

5 Ipswich Avenue,
Loughton,
Essex,
IG10 4BX

10th June 19__

Miss Ann Howard,
Publicity Director,
Messrs Bower & Cassidy,
11 Peartree Road,
London, W1M 2AD

Dear Miss Howard,

I am writing to ask you whether you have any vacancies for a publicity assistant. I have worked as a publicity assistant in the public relations departments of two local authorities and have experience of all aspects of local government publicity work. Nevertheless I have always had ambitions to work in publishing and am particularly interested in your company's list of cookery and gardening books.

I realize that I would have to start at the bottom but I am anxious to learn about all aspects of publishing and appreciate that working in such a well-respected publishing firm as Bower & Cassidy would be the best way to gain experience.

Yours sincerely,

Jane Price

Letter requesting job application form

17 Dartmouth Avenue,
Harlow,
Essex,
H2 4JJ

11th December 19___

The Chief Personnel Manager,
Evans and Buchanan,
32 Banbury Road,
Harlow, Essex
H2 3GL.

Dear Sir,

I have seeen your advertisement for an accounts clerk in *The Harlow Bugle* and should be grateful if you would send me an application form for the post.

Yours faithfully,

F. Lewis

Letter inviting candidate to attend job interview

Marshall, Tucker & Co.,
7 High Street,
London NW5 6RT

Our reference: MPT/PC   Tel No 01-000 0000

Mr James Drummond
Flat 2
7 Berners Way
London NW3 4RF

12 November, 19__

Dear Mr Drummond

With reference to your recent application for the post of Production Controller with this company, I should be pleased if you would come for an interview on Friday 28 November at 9.30 a.m. You should ask for Mrs Barton at the Reception Desk.

Could you please telephone Mrs Barton on extension 34 to confirm that you are able to attend and whether you are willing for a reference from your present employer to be taken up at this stage.

Yours sincerely

B Brooks
Personnel Department

Letter to job applicant who has not been offered a post

Our ref: APP/56/G

West Country Foods Ltd
12 Grosvenor Street
Exeter
Devon
EX4 5BN
Tel: 00000

Mr James Osborne
14 Bromley Way
Exeter
Devon
EX3 8UH

19 December 19__

Dear Mr Osborne

CHIEF BUYER

Further to your interview for the above post, I am writing to confirm that we have offered the post to another candidate. Thank you for your interest in the position and for attending the interviews.

Yours sincerely

Sarah Rae
Personnel Co-ordinator

Letter of appointment to a post

Samuel N. Green Ltd.,
18 Marsden Avenue,
ASHBY-DE-LA-ZOUCH,
Leicestershire
LE3 1AB
Telephone: Ashby-de-la-Zouch
(031-48) 61736

Our ref: 985/B   5th May 19__

Ms O Simmonds,
5 Wakeling Crescent,
Melton Mowbray,
Leicestershire
LE3 12B

Dear Ms Simmonds,

   Following your recent interview, I am pleased to
confirm your appointment to the position of Typing
Pool Supervisor with Samuel N. Green Ltd at a salary
of £X a year, terminable by one month's written notice
on either side. You will be entitled to 25 days paid
annual holiday. Our office hours are from 9.30 am to
5.30 pm from Monday to Friday.

   I understand that you can join us on Monday 16th
June and look forward to seeing you at 9.30 am on that
day. If there is any other information which you need,
please do not hesitate to telephone me or my secretary.

Yours sincerely

Patsy Green
Personnel Director

Letter accepting a post

5 Morrison Court,
Station Road,
Shooters Hill,
London, SE18 9LK.

M. James Esq.,
Personnel Manager,
Parsons Tools Ltd.,
5 Empire Way,
Deptford, London, SE8 3PR

5th September 19___

Dear Mr James,

Thank you for your letter of 3rd September offering me the post of Export Sales Manager.

I am very pleased to accept the offer and hope to be able to take up my post on 10th November. As you are aware, I have to give my present employers two months' notice.

Yours sincerely,

Andrew Butt

Letter accepting a post but raising queries

'Little Pines'
9 Pinetree Hill
Cheltenham Gloucestershire
GL53 1JN

7th September 19___

Personnel Officer
Basil and Taylor Ltd
15 Metropolitan Street
Worcester
WR4 5TG

Dear Sir

Thank you for you letter of 4th September, offering me the post of Sales Manager.

A number of points were raised at my interview and I should like to be sure that I have understood them correctly:

1. My salary will be £X per annum with a five per cent bonus for achieving specified sales figures over a year.

2. I will receive £X towards my relocation expenses.

3. Every other year I will be provided with a new company car for business and private use.

I hope you will be able to confirm these points and providing you can do so I shall be pleased to accept your offer and shall look forward to starting work with you on 1st November.

Yours faithfully

F. J. SANDERS

Giving names of referees when applying for a job

Prospective employers may ask for the names of two or more referees who will testify to your suitability for the job in question, your education and training or your character. Normally one of these should be your present employer and all referees should be people you know well. They should also be people whose opinions will carry weight, who are respected in their professions or in the community. Before giving anyone's name as a referee you should of course get their consent.

Some firms will take up references only if they intend to offer a candidate the job in question and if you would rather not tell your present employer that you are looking for a new job, you can ask that this reference should only be taken up if a job is to be offered to you.

Letter to previous employer applying for a reference

5 Maddison House,
Bridge Street,
Aldershot,
Hants.

7th November 19___

Mr A Archer,
Archer & Sons,
27 Ferry Parade,
Petersfield,
Hants.

Dear Mr Archer,

I have just been offered the post of Senior Auditor with Cowplain Borough Council and should be most grateful if you would give me reference which I could send to my new employers. Would you please comment on the standard of my work, my abilities and my character.

Yours sincerely,

George Gilbert

Letter to present employer applying for a reference

98 Magpie Lane
Southport
Merseyside

PRIVATE AND CONFIDENTIAL   PR8 1RB
A. K. Bishop Esq.,   23 May 19___
Manager,
Grove Machinery,
12-16 Chubb Row,
Southport, Merseyside,
PR8 3FZ

Dear Mr Bishop,

I am applying for a post as senior engineer at Bryant Tools factory in Poole and should be most grateful if you would allow me to give your name as a referee.

Although I am very happy with Grove Machinery, the Bryant Tools position would be a considerable advance for me in terms of both status and salary.

If I do not succeed in obtaining the position, I hope that you will appreciate that it was a logical application for me to make and that I am not dissatisfied with my job here.

Yours sincerely,

M. T. Hodge

Resigning from a job

If you are resigning from your job because you have been offered other employment, you would be well advised to wait till you have the offer of the new job in writing before resigning from your present post. Once you are sure that the terms of employment such as salary, job title, responsibilities, holiday entitlement and job location are as you understood them, you must write a letter of resignation from your present job, giving the required amount of notice as specified in your contract of employment.

No matter why you are leaving your job, you must give the necessary notice and you should always resign graciously – do not write an impolite letter you may afterwards regret nor attempt to settle old scores. You never know when you may need advice or a reference from a former employer. If you have been unhappy in your job you should still write a polite, though brief letter such as the one below.

Letter of resignation from a job (1)

16 Rock Lane,
Swindon, SN2 4RX

J. Harris Esq
Wyante Sales Ltd
4 Lower Road   4th October 19__
Swindon SN4 5RF

Dear Mr Harris,

I have been offered a very good job as Secretary to the
Managing Director of a local manufacturing company
and I write therefore to give you formal notice that I
will be terminating my employment with you on 4th
November.

Yours sincerely

Georgina Miller

Letter of resignation from a job (2)

If you have always been happy with your work, you may wish to write a warmer, less formal letter, terminating your employment.

38 Lang Street,
Newport, Gwent,
NP5 1TY
Tel: 56370

Mrs P Harrington
John Rushton & Son
14 Highview Lane
Newport, Gwent
NP4 3RF

7th April 19___

Dear Mrs Harrington,

I am writing to inform you that I have just been appointed senior secretary at Brooker and Company and that I will therefore be terminating my employment with you at the end of May.

I have much enjoyed my work at Rushtons over the past three years and I am sure the excellent training you gave me was instrumental in my getting this new job.

Yours sincerely

Janet Bartholomew

Letter of resignation from a job (3)

If you are resigning because you have not been given the salary increase or promotion you feel you deserve, you can explain why you are leaving, but do so tactfully and retain the goodwill of your employers. Who knows, they might even change their mind and offer you that seat on the Board!

> 178 Northern Lane,
> Wakefield,
> W. Yorks. WF2 3BN
>
> 30th May 19__

Mr Gerald Tiny
Harper Designs Ltd
35 The Broadway
Wakefield
W. Yorks WF4 7TY

Dear Mr Tiny

I have considered what you have said to me at our meeting on Thursday and I appreciate that because the export market is so difficult at the moment you cannot offer me the salary increase I feel my qualifications and experience as export assistant deserve.

I have therefore decided to accept the job I have been offered by Graham and Williams. I feel they can offer me much better financial prospects and that I would be more likely to be promoted. I am taking this step with reluctance because I enjoy my work with you and get on with my colleagues in the Export Department.

I should be grateful if you would allow me to leave in four weeks, so that I can take up my new post on 1st July.

Yours sincerely

Magnus Young

Letter replying to a letter of resignation

Just as an employee should always try to resign graciously, whatever his or her personal feelings may be, an employer too, should receive and reply to a letter of resignation in a tactful way.

Harper Designs Limited
35 The Broadway
Wakefield
W. Yorks WF4 7TY

Mr Magnus Young
178 Northern Lane
Wakefield W. Yorks
WF2 3BN

1st June 19___

Dear Mr Young,

Thank you for your letter of 30th May. I am sorry to learn that you are leaving this Company after having given us such excellent service for the past three years. Nevertheless we will of course allow you to leave at the end of the month, so you can take up your new post, and we wish you well in the future.

Yours sincerely,

G. Tiny
Managing Director

Giving references

It is wise to send references to a named person, wherever possible, and to mark your envelope 'Confidential'.

If you know of any serious reason why a person would not be suitable for a job, you should tell the prospective employer that you cannot recommend that person. In the main, however, it is best not to give specific reasons but rather to answer only the questions asked by the prospective employer. He or she will be able to draw his or her own conclusions from your reticence.

Employers are entitled to refuse to give a reference to a member of staff who is leaving their employ but if the employer does give a reference it must be a fair one, written without malice.

Of course, if you think highly of the person in question you should point out their good qualities to the prospective employer, keeping your comments relevant to the job in question.

Letter taking up a reference

R. J. Adams Ltd
13 Brook Street
Northampton
NN5 6TL

A. R. Bolting Esq
J. P. Symes (Footwear) Ltd
7 Lington Road
Wakefield
West Yorkshire
WF6 3JH

6th January 19___

Dear Mr Bolting,

Mr C. J. Clarke, who is a salesman with your firm, has applied for the position of Sales Manager with us.

We should be glad if you would kindly let us know, in confidence, your opinion of his character and ability and his relations with other members of your staff.

A short list of the applicants has been prepared, and as the Directors meet to make the appointment on 16th January, it would be appreciated if we could have your reply by 13th January at the latest.

Yours sincerely,

Margaret Neville
Personnel Officer

Letter giving favourable reference

J. P. Symes (Footwear) Ltd,
7 Lington Road
Wakefield
West Yorkshire
WF6 3JH

<u>Confidential</u>

Ms Margaret Neville
Personnel Officer
R. J. Adams Ltd
13 Brook Street
Northampton
NN5 6TL

9th January 19___

Dear Ms Neville

In reply to your letter of 6th January, we are pleased to
inform you that Mr Charles Clarke has been a
valuable member of our sales team for the last four
years. During that time he has greatly assisted the
building up of our sales and has made a number of very
useful contacts. He is a thoroughly efficient, honest
and capable member of our staff. We would be very
sorry to lose him, even though we realise his
qualifications and experience are such as to merit
promotion. If you secure him as a member of your staff
we are sure you will be satisfied with your choice.

Yours sincerely

G. P. Bland
Manager

Letter giving qualified reference

Bartlet and Simpson
100 Crowther Street
Penzance
Cornwall
TR4 5HN

15th February 19__

A. Bogle Esq
Messrs Pepper & Green
23 Meridian Way
Newquay
Cornwall
TR18 7HB

Dear Mr Bogle,

Miss B. Mills, who was an architectural assistant
in this office for three years, has asked me to give her a
reference. Although Miss Mills is very intelligent and
not afraid of work she did occasionally make some
elementary errors which I am sure she would not have
made had she shown greater concentration. This may
have happened because she was in need of a change
and I am sure that she would give you satisfactory
service.

Yours sincerely,

Giles Bartlet

Letter refusing a reference (1)

Carlisle Ltd.,
5 Hardwick Close,
Hayes, Middlesex
UB5 4HF

<u>PRIVATE AND CONFIDENTIAL</u>

J. T. Strickland Esq.,
Personnel Manager,
Collier and Streeting Ltd.,
10 Peverley Arcade,
Hayes,
Middlesex UB5 3DS

16th May 19

Dear Mr Strickland,

In reply to your letter of 12th March, enquiring about Mr Frederick Castleton, I regret that I am unable to recommend him to you and told him so when he left us. In the circumstances I prefer to say nothing more.

Yours sincerely,

J. J. Wells,
Manager.

Letter refusing a reference (2)

Clair's Hairdressing
2 Ashford Road
Lymington
Hampshire SO4 7AR

PRIVATE AND CONFIDENTIAL
Mrs J Tyler
"Curlers" Hairdressing
7 Milton Walk
Lyndhurst
Hampshire
SO4 5RF

6th April 19__

Dear Mrs Tyler,

Thank you for your letter of 4th April asking for a reference for Emma Johnstone. Ms Johnstone only worked here for some six months and I am afraid I did not know her well enough to be of use to you.

Yours sincerely

Cathy Bromley (Ms)

Open reference – favourable

To whom it may concern:

Mr Alan Hennessy has worked in our Sales Department for the last five years during which time he has greatly contributed to the success of the firm. He got on extremely well with the other members of staff and I shall be sorry to lose his services.

He is leaving us because he wishes to move back to the North to be near his elderly parents. It gives me pleasure to recommend him wholeheartedly for any post where his abilities can be used to advantage.

M. P. Stanton
Managing Director

Open reference for person not highly regarded

To whom it may concern:

Mr Alan Hennessy is leaving this Company because he is looking for a post with a higher salary than we are willing to pay. He has worked here for the past three years and we have found his work satisfactory. We wish him well in his future employment.

J. Harris
Works Manager

3 General business letters

Sending circular letters

The personal effect can be heightened, and the whole process greatly eased, by using a word processor for such letters. All you need to do is to type in the individual's name and address at the top of the standard letter, and then print out a copy for each addressee. Mail order lists of customer addresses can be word processed in a similar way and whole lists of customers printed out with minimal effort.

Circular letter concerning new ownership of business

Fenner Newsagents
Head Office 135 Park Street
Southend-on-Sea
SS3 8JG

Dear Customer,

As of 4th August, as you are probably aware, we shall have taken The Parade Newsagents, 78 Swallow Street, Eastleigh, under our wing.

We hope that you will be satisfied with our service, as we are sure you have been with the previous owners, Mr and Mrs Jameson.

The purpose of this letter is to introduce ourselves to you and to explain the mechanics of our Company.

As you are aware, in these inflationary times, money is very restricted and for this reason we would inform you that our maximum credit on home deliveries is four weeks. We regret that any accounts unpaid after four weeks will cease to receive deliveries. Whilst we would prefer accounts to be settled each week we realise this is not always possible.

We are sure we can rely on your help and cooperation in this matter and look forward to many happy years of serving you.

Yours sincerely,

J. G. Fenner

Circular letter about setting up new branch

ANDERSON AND FIELDING LTD

2-4 Briggs Street,
Walthamstow,
London, E17 9PR

01-520 0000

19th June 19___

Dear Sir

The demand for our products in south London has been increasing steadily over the past few years and we have now opened a showroom at 13 Brenner Road, Lewisham, SE13 9QR. Telephone 01-858 0000. The new showroom will make it easy for you to examine our wide range of high quality cutlery and glassware.

Mr Jonathan Black, who has been known to most of our customers for a number of years, has been appointed Manager of the showroom, and he will be delighted to help you when you call.

Yours faithfully
ANDERSON AND FIELDING LTD.

A. Sillett
Director

Circular letter about admission of new partner

Young and Freeman Ltd
5 Hall Street
Bournemouth
Dorset
BH2 5HR
15th February 19__

Addressee

Dear Mr   ,

We are delighted to announce that as from
1st March 19   we are taking into partnership
Mr Donald B. Wilson, who has been our Production
Manager for the last ten years and who has a wide
grasp of all facets of our business.

Mr Wilson will continue to act as Production
Manager for the time being, and we feel that now he
has become a partner, his initiative and drive will be
brought into the wider problems of our business.

Yours sincerely,
YOUNG & FREEMAN

L. Young

Letter introducing representative to prospective customer (1)

Morrison and French Ltd
Waverley Mills
Sheffield
S. Yorkshire S10 5DX

Our ref: JV/CF   10th February 19__

G. T. Baxter Esq.,
13 Weymouth Terrace,
Catford, SE6 9PC

Dear Mr Baxter,

This is to introduce Mr O. D. Oliver, B.Sc., who is a representative of Partridge, Nash Ltd.

Mr Oliver intends to visit south London in the near future to interview a number of firms, and I have suggested that he make the first call on you because I feel sure you can give him some useful information on the district.

You will find Mr Oliver a very pleasant young man. I know I can rely on you to give him all the help you can.

With best wishes,
Yours sincerely,

James P. C. French

Letter introducing representative to prospective customer (2)

It is a good idea for a director or perhaps the sales manager of an organization to write a letter of introduction to a prospective customer who he or she knows, introducing another member of the firm, for example a salesperson.

> Northumbria Advertising Services Ltd
> 78 Osborne Villas
> Newcastle upon Tyne
> Tyne and Wear NE2 1NT

Mr Peter Brown
Browns Ltd
New Bridge Lane
Barnard Castle
Co. Durham
DL4 5EB

27th August 19__

Dear Mr Brown

We think we can help you spend your advertising budget more effectively. Will you have time to see our Mr Oldham for a few minutes one day next week? He will not need more than about fifteen minutes and you will be able to judge for yourself how we can be of use to you. I shall be delighted if we can be of service to you in any way.

> Yours sincerely
>
>
> V. Harper
> Managing Director

Letter of thanks for introduction
for representative

Partridge, Nash Ltd,
Market Place,
Scunthorpe,
South Humberside,
DN15 7DF

Mr James P. C. French
Morrison and French Ltd
Waverley Mills
Sheffield
South Yorkshire
S10 5DX

12 March 19___

Dear Mr French

This is to thank you very much for the letter of
introduction you wrote for our representative,
Mr Oliver, when he recently made a trip to south
London. Your friend Mr Baxter gave him a very warm
welcome and much good advice. We are most grateful
for the meetings Mr Baxter arranged for him, which
have resulted in some valuable business contacts.

I am writing to tell Mr Baxter how much we
appreciated his help. I know he is an extremely busy
man, and this makes me all the more grateful to him
for so kindly sparing the time to see our
representative.

Yours sincerely

J. Woodcock
Sales Manager (South-East)

Letter opening company's bank account

William Smithson & Co. Ltd.
169 Reading Lane
Bournemouth
Dorset
BH2 5HR

20th October 19___

The Manager
National Bank Ltd
Peter Lane
Bournemouth
Dorset
BH2 5HR

Dear Sir

Following our meeting on 2nd October, I confirm that
my Company wish to open an account with your bank
and enclose:

Copy of the Resolution appointing National Bank Ltd.
as the Company's Bankers, authenticated by the
Chairman, together with specimen signatures of
Mr Charles D. Smithson, Managing Director, and that
of my own, S. J. Penfold, Secretary;

Printed copies of the Company's memorandum and
Articles of Association;

The Company's Certificate of Incorporation; and

The Company's Certificate to Commence Business.

Will you please return the two latter documents after
you have inspected them.

Our Office Manager, Mr D. B. Jones, will be calling at the bank within the next few days or so to obtain a cheque book and paying-in book.

Yours faithfully
for WILLIAM SMITHSON & CO LTD

S. J. Penfold
Secretary

Encs/6

Letter asking bank to stop payment of cheque

William Smithson & Co. Ltd.
169 Reading Lane
Bournemouth
Dorset
BH2 5HR

6th February 19___

The Manager
National Bank Ltd
Peter Lane
Bournemouth
Dorset
BH2 5HR

Dear Sir

I confirm my telephone converstion with you this
morning when I asked you to stop payment of a cheque,
details of which are as follows:

Cheque No.	34/3876
Date:	5th February 19___
Payee:	James Martin
Drawer:	p.p. William Smithson & Co
	Charles D. Smithson,
	Managing Director.

Yours faithfully
for WILLIAM SMITHSON & CO LTD

S. J. Penfold
Secretary

Application for a commission agent

It is common practice for companies to use commission agents to conduct business in foreign countries. Unlike an ordinary agent, a commission agent buys and sells in his own name, receiving a percentage of the price of the goods – a commission – for his service. This is normally less expensive for a company than sending one of its own sales force abroad, and a native of any country will usually have better business contacts and know the market more thoroughly than a foreigner will.

Where a company is doubtful about the financial status of prospective customers abroad, it is common practice to appoint a *del credere* agent who will guarantee payment for the goods supplied. To compensate the agent for the extra risk he undertakes he is paid an extra commission known as a *del credere* commission.

Letter of application for a commission agent

> Plaza Orientale
> Rio De Janeiro
> Brazil

Green & Jackson (Electrical Appliances) Ltd.,
  14 Quigley Parade
    Birmingham
      B10 4QR   28th May 19___

Dear Sirs,

    I am informed by my bankers, R. Gonzales Compania that you need an agent for your products in Brazil. Subject to satisfactory terms and conditions, I should be very happy to represent you.

Over a period of twelve years I have established an excellent sales organization and have first-class business connections throughout the country. I represent three of the foremost American electrical companies. Some of their products are similar to your own goods – though not necessarily competitive. I am convinced there would be a promising market for your products, so long as the quality, prices and packing were right. Provided we could agree upon satisfactory commission and terms of payment, I would undertake to guarantee payment of the accounts due on orders placed through me.

I am sure an agency for marketing your electrical appliances in Brazil would benefit both of us and I look forward to hearing from you.

Yours faithfully,

Z. Lopez

Letter to a prospective agent (1)

Mitchell and Norman Ltd
Fashion Knitwear,
75 Berkshire Way,
Coventry, CV2 3RT

Monsieur P. Ferlin,
27 rue Pierre Curie,
CONTREXEVILLE   5th April 19___

Dear Mr Ferlin,

We think we could sell far more of our high quality English and Scottish knitwear in France and we are therefore looking for an agent to represent us.
Your firm has been recommended to us and we would like to offer you sole agency in France.

I enclose an illustrated catalogue and price list so that you can see the wide range of garments we make. Our cashmere pullovers represent especially good value. We will let you have samples if you wish to see them.

We should like to pay you a commission of 15% of the invoice value of the orders you take; we would pay this quarterly. We could supply on consignment but would prefer to pay on a commission basis. We will contribute £0000 towards an advertising campaign.

We look forward to hearing from you.

Yours sincerely

N. G. Mitchell
EXPORT DIRECTOR

(Enclosures)

Letter to a prospective agent (2)

Mitchell and Norman Ltd
   Fashion Knitwear,
75 Berkshire Way,
Coventry, CV2 3RT

Monsieur P. Ferlin,
27 rue Pierre Curie,
CONTREXEVILLE   14th April 19___

Dear Mr Ferlin,

    Thank you for your letter of 10th April about the French agency. We are delighted you think our products should sell well in your country.

    These are the points we have agreed on:

1.   You will operate as our sole agents in France.
2.   You will receive two samples of each new line we introduce.
3.   You will be paid 15% commission on the invoice value of the orders you get.
4.   You will be paid quarterly and will send your account ten days before payment is due.
5.   We agree to contribute £0000 towards an advertising campaign in women's magazines this autumn. You will send us your proposals and a 'rough' of the advertisement.
6.   We will review the arrangements again after twelve months.

    Please let me know if you agree with all these conditions. If so, I will let you have a draft agreement for your signature.

Yours sincerely,

N. G. Mitchell
EXPORT DIRECTOR

Letter about disposal of a business

THORNTON AND COOKE LTD
High Field
Oxford OX2 4JJ
Tel: 00000

Mr J. W. Stanton,
Stanton's Stores
Hall Lane
Oxford
OX5 8FD

JKT/GFC

1st July 19___

Dear Mr Stanton,

I am sorry to tell you that I have decided to take an
early retirement, because of my poor health.
As from 1st September the warehouse will be closed.
Between now and that date we will be selling the
stock, shopfittings and some office machinery at very
competitive prices for cash. If you are interested do
come and inspect the items on sale as soon as possible.
I am sure you will find some real bargains here.

May I also take this opportunity of thanking you
for your past custom and wishing you much success in
the future.

With good wishes,
Yours sincerely,

James K. Thornton

Writing letters of congratulations

These are very personal letters and are best hand-written rather than typed. A hand-written letter suggests that the writer has spent some time and effort in writing and also seems more friendly.

Letter of congratulations (1)

> Kettle & Couzens Ltd
> 395 Bickton Road
> London SW6 5TG
>
> 17th June 19___

Dear Paul and Louise

Everyone here at Kettle & Couzens was thrilled to hear of your marriage and we all send you our congratulations.

You certainly know how to keep a secret – in fact you kept so quiet about it that we had no idea the sales department and the production department were planning to join forces.

We have all subscribed to buy you this small gift which we hope you will find useful in your new home. It comes with all our good wishes for your happiness.

> Yours sincerely,

Letter of congratulation (2)

If you hear of a business associate's success in obtaining an important post, or of passing a professional examination, or receiving an award, you may wish to drop him or her a short friendly note. However, you should always convey the impression that the success was no more than you expected and was very much deserved. Never suggest that it was a surprise to you!

Spender & Price Ltd
7 Parker Street
London E10 7BB

4th October 19__

Dear Michael

I was delighted to see you have been promoted to Chief Accountant. I saw the announcement in the trade press and felt that I had to drop you this line, short though it is.

With every good wish,
Yours sincerely,

Writing letters of condolence

Here again, a handwritten letter is called for. Keep your letter fairly brief and do not mention any other subject in your letter – even if there are some urgent points you really need to discuss with the person you are writing to. Avoid flowery language and euphemisms – just use the words of everyday speech to express the sorrow you are feeling. Do not offer help unless you are really willing to give it.

Letter of condolence (1)
(to the widow of a former employee)

> Spender & Price Ltd
> 7 Parker Street
> London E10 7BB
>
> 15th July 19__

Dear Mrs Fisher,

It was with great sorrow that I learned of the death of your husband and I know my feelings will be shared by everyone who worked with him during his many years with the firm.

Please accept the sympathy of all your husband's former colleagues here, and of myself personally.

> Yours very sincerely,

Letter of condolence (2)
(to an employee)

Taylor & Brown Ltd
Yale Road
Stourbridge
West Midlands
DY8 1QS

Tel: 67599

12th February 19__

Dear Miss Frost,

I was very shocked to hear of the sudden death of your mother and offer you my sympathy in your loss.

I am sure you will have many personal matters to attend to, so I shall certainly not expect to see you at the office for the next couple of weeks. Please do not worry about your work at all. However, if you have any personal worries or if there is an immediate difficulty in your situation in which the Company might be able to help, do let me know.

Yours very truly,

4 Accounts department correspondence

The accounts department of a business or organization is responsible primarily for the correspondence concerning payment of accounts, outstanding accounts and collection of debts, queries about discount and terms, discrepancies in invoices, and the granting of credit.

Invoices

An invoice is a document which a seller sends to a purchaser. It shows the amount payable and gives details of the goods sold. The layout of invoices may vary from firm to firm but always includes the name and address of the seller and the VAT registration number, tax point and type of supply if the seller is registered for VAT. It may also show the purchaser's order number, the method of dispatch and the terms of payment.

A Pro Forma invoice is an invoice sent to cover goods sent on consignment, or on approval, or where payment is required in advance (for example when the purchaser does not have an account with the supplier), or it is sometimes used as a quotation.

Example of invoice

Invoice

FROM: Superphone Ltd
Superphone House
2 Park Square
Lowestoft
Suffolk
NR65 0BN

TO: Mr J Swan,
9 Bridge Street,
King's Lynn,
Norfolk
PE23 7RD

Ref: T56g   Vat. No. 000 0000 00
Tax Point

	£	p	@	£	p
			VAT		
TO: Rent for entrance speaker system from 1.1.19 to 31.12.19	36	00			
Due on or before 1st January 19___					
	36	00	15%	5	40
				36	00
DATE 15.12.19___ E. & O.E.				41	00

89

Credit notes

A credit note is a document which is sent to a buyer by a seller to cancel an incorrect invoice or rectify it, or to acknowledge receipt of goods, packing cases etc. returned by the buyer and allow credit for them. Credit notes are usually printed and typed in red.

A supplier who credits his customer for services or goods which are subject to VAT must issue a VAT credit note, which will give the VAT registration number of the supplier, the amount credited for each item, the rate of VAT and the amount of VAT credited.

Example of credit note

Credit by

Crowthers Ltd	Tel: 00000
Port Road	Telex: 00000
Reading	VAT Reg. No. 00000
Berks	
RG7 4RU	20 April 19___

Swans Ltd
97 Dukes Road
Pangbourne
Berkshire
RG8 5AR

Credit Note No. 983

Your order Number	*Description*	£	p
89/G/22/6	To overcharging:		
	30 1507@£0.35	10	50
With apologies			

Debit notes

A debit note is sent by a seller to a buyer to rectify an undercharge on an invoice. Unlike the credit note, it is not printed in red.

Statement of Account

Statements are sent at regular intervals, usually each month, by an organization to each of its customers, summarizing the month's transactions. The statement shows any balance brought forward from the previous month, the date and amount of invoices sent, credit notes sent and payments received. A debtor can check his own ledger against the particulars in the statement so that any errors can be discovered.

A Statement of Account can be set out in various ways but the most common form is the debit/credit and balance style, shown below. The last amount shown in the 'Balance' column is the amount to be paid.

Example of a Statement of Account

Crowthers Ltd   Tel: 00000
Port Road   Telex: 00000
Reading   VAT Reg. No. 00000
Berks   Tax Point:
RG7 4RU

STATEMENT

Date	Ref No.	Debit	Credit	Balance
4.4.19__	70340	105.00		105.00
25.3.19__	80100	65.50		170.50
2.4.19__	C/N 107		20.00	150.50
10.4.19__	82903	200.00		350.50
		Terms 30 days		
		Amount due		350.50

Overdue accounts

You can help to avoid the income loss caused by 'bad-payers' if you send out your invoices immediately by first-class post and include all invoices on a monthly statement. But there will certainly be some 'bad-payers'.

Remember that many people often do not settle accounts quickly because they are not as well organized as they should be. It is therefore best initially to regard everyone as honest rather than automatically to assume the worst. Your first reminder letter should thus assume that the account has been overlooked and you should normally wait until you have sent several unsuccessful reminder letters before threatening legal action, as you should always aim at retaining the goodwill of your customers. Moreover, if your reminder letters are well-written you may even add to your goodwill.

nay either send a letter like the one below or you
prefer to send a statement of account overprinted
the words *"Second Application"* or *"This statement contains items which are now overdue"*.

BAXTER & TIBBLE LTD
72 Regent's Valley
Greenwich
London SE10 6RS

01-692 0000

14th April 19—

Ref: BM/GTB

A. Howard Furnishing Ltd
21 Tulsa Avenue
Folkestone
Kent FO3 1EH

Dear Sirs,

May we remind you that you have not yet settled
our account for £105.41 due on 31st March 19—.

In case the invoice has gone astray, we enclose a
copy Statement of Account and should be grateful if
you would let us have your cheque in payment by
return of post.

Yours faithfully,
for BAXTER & TIBBLE LTD

B. Moy
Accountant

Enc.

Letter about overdue account – first reminder (2)

Here is another way of phrasing this letter, which again gives your customer the benefit of the doubt and assumes that he has not paid because of an oversight rather than because he cannot pay or because he is trying to avoid paying you. Give your customer a loophole and so keep his goodwill.

BAXTER & TIBBLE LTD
72 Regent's Valley
Greenwich
London SE10 6RS

01-692 0000

14th April 19__

Ref: BM/GTB

A. Howard Furnishing Ltd
21 Tulsa Avenue
Folkestone
Kent FO3 1EH

Dear Sirs,

We note that your Accounts Department has still not settled our account for £105.41. As you know, our conditions of sale include payment within thirty days of our invoice and I imagine the delay has occurred because this is your busiest trading season. Nevertheless, this account was due on 31st March and we would much appreciate settlement by return.

Yours faithfully,
for BAXTER & TIBBLE LTD

B. Moy
Accountant

Letter about overdue account – second reminder

If the account remains unpaid, you might consider telephoning your customer to establish there are no complaints. If you can get him to promise a date for payment, confirm this by letter. Otherwise you can write him a letter like the one below.

BAXTER & TIBBLE LTD
72 Regent's Valley
Greenwich
London SE10 6RS

01-692 0000

24th April 19___

Ref: BM/GTB

A. Howard Furnishing Ltd
21 Tulsa Avenue
Folkestone
Kent FO3 1EH

Dear Sirs,

We are surprised that we have received no reply from you to our letter of 14th April asking for payment of our account for £105.41.

In the circumstances we must suspend further delivery of goods to you and ask you to let us have your cheque by return of post.

Yours faithfully,
for BAXTER & TIBBLE LTD

B. Moy
Accountant

Letter about overdue account – third reminder

BAXTER & TIBBLE LTD
72 Regent's Valley
Greenwich
London SE10 6RS

01-692 0000

24th May 19__

Ref: BM/GTB

A. Howard Furnishing Ltd
21 Tulsa Avenue
Folkestone
Kent FO3 1EH

Dear Sirs,

We are extremely concerned that you have not
replied to our letters of the 14th and 24th April
regarding our outstanding account for £105.41 which
was due on 31st March. It is only because we value
your goodwill that we have not referred the matter to
our debt collectors. If, however, you do not settle the
account within seven days, we shall reluctantly have
to do so.

Yours faithfully,
for BAXTER & TIBBLE LTD

B. Moy
Accountant

Letter about overdue account – fourth reminder

If you are dealing with a particularly valuable customer you might wish to send another reminder letter, before passing the matter to debt collectors. It would be a good idea to send this letter by recorded delivery.

BAXTER & TIBBLE LTD
72 Regent's Valley
Greenwich
London SE10 6RS

01-692 0000

31st May 19___

Ref: BM/GTB

A. Howard Furnishing Ltd
21 Tulsa Avenue
Folkestone
Kent FO3 1EH

Dear Sirs,

I am surprised to note that despite our letter dated 24th May, we have still not received your cheque for £105.41. I therefore have to inform you that your account will be passed to our debt collectors at the end of this week, at which point interest and legal charges will also become due.

Yours faithfully,
for BAXTER & TIBBLE LTD

B. Moy
Accountant

Letter about overdue account – final reminder

BAXTER & TIBBLE LTD
72 Regent's Valley
Greenwich
London SE10 6RS

01-692 0000

31st May 19___

Ref: BM/GTB

A. Howard Furnishing Ltd
21 Tulsa Avenue
Folkestone
Kent FO3 1EH

Dear Sirs,

Since we have received no reply from you to our letters of 14th and 24th April and 24th and 31st May, requesting payment of our March account for £105.41, we have reluctantly referred the matter to our debt collectors.

> Yours faithfully,
> for BAXTER & TIBBLE LTD
>
>
> B. Moy
> Accountant

Letter asking for more time to pay account

A. Howard Furnishing Ltd
21 Tulsa Avenue
Folkestone
Kent

Your ref: BM/GTB   FO3 1EH

Our ref: OD/BB/255   Telephone: 000000

<u>For the attention of</u>   2nd June 19__
  <u>Mr B. Moy</u>

Baxter & Tibble Ltd
72 Regent's Valley
Greenwich
London
SE10 6RS

Dear Sirs,

We are very sorry that we have not replied earlier to your letters requesting payment of your March account for £105.41.

However, we have been passing through a difficult trading period because of the current recession and have severe cash-flow problems. Although we had hoped to clear your account, the best we can do at the moment is to let you have the enclosed cheque for £40.00 on account and to ask you to give us further time in which to settle the balance.

As our trading position appears to be improving, we should be able to clear our debt within the next few weeks. In the meantime, we should be most grateful if you would let us know whether you would be prepared to lift your suspension of further deliveries to us.

Once again, we apologise for any inconvenience we have caused.

Yours faithfully,

(Miss) A. Howard
Director

Letter replying to above

BAXTER & TIBBLE LTD
72 Regent's Valley
Greenwich
London SE10 6RS

01-629 0000

6th June 19___

Your ref: OD/BB/255

Our ref: BM/GTB

A. Howard Furnishing Ltd
21 Tulsa Avenue
Folkestone
Kent
FO3 1EH

Dear Sirs,

Thank you for your letter of 2nd, enclosing your cheque for £40 on account.

Though we are sorry to hear that you are having difficulty collecting the amounts due to you from your own customers we do not feel we should be expected to bear the burden of this. However, because of your long association with us and your previous good credit record we do not wish to press you unduly, especially as you expect to be able to settle your account within the next few weeks.

In the meantime we will be glad to supply goods to you on a cash with order basis and to allow you an additional 2½% discount in lieu of credit.

We hope you will agree to this arrangement and that you will be able to settle your account by the end of next month. We would be sorry to have to close your account or to place the matter in the hands of our debt collectors.

Yours faithfully,
for BAXTER & TIBBLE LTD

B. Moy
Accountant

Letter apologizing that invoice has not been paid

5th March 19___

Stags Ltd,
8 Royal Drive,
Preston, Lancashire
PR5 3JX

K. R. Burton Esq
Credit Manager
Birch & Hawk Ltd
Unit 4
Belling Trading Estate
Hastings
East Sussex
TN38 9NB

Tel: Preston 00000

Dear Sir

I received this morning your letter of 27th February containing two outstanding invoices for last November.

I am at a loss to understand why these have not been paid, and I have instructed our Accounts Department to look into this matter immediately.

Yours faithfully

Owen Milford

Refusing requests for special terms or extra credit

Letters refusing a request for special terms or extra credit must be written with great care so that you do not cause offence and lose a customer. Explain why you are refusing the request and if possible tell your correspondent the circumstances under which you might be able to help him.

Letter refusing request for special terms

SWIFT ELECTRICAL SUPPLIES LTD
9 Argyle Street
Halifax
HX1 2TY

Telephone: Halifax 0000

19th January 19—

T. L. Barker Ltd
Providence Way
Halifax
HX6 7GH

Dear Sirs,

We are sorry to learn from your letter of 16th January that you find our quotation for Zenith Radio Cassette Players was too high.

We have carefully considered your request for an additional discount bearing in mind the large amount of business you have done with us recently but we regret that this would leave us with little or no profit.

Despite the rise in the cost of raw material and labour charges we have kept our prices at the same level as last spring and we feel our quotation was extremely competitive. We are very sorry that we cannot allow you the special discount you requested.

I do hope you will appreciate our position and that we can look forward to supplying the goods for which we quoted.

Yours faithfully

J. C. Millwood

Example of form for customer wanting to open account

Before opening an account for prospective customer you will need to make sure he is credit-worthy. This is the type of form you might devise which your customer can complete.

REQUEST TO OPEN A CREDIT ACCOUNT

Name or Trading Style

Name of Proprietor

Full statement address

Telephone number

Delivery address

Nature of Business
(wholesaler/retailer)

Associated Companies

Name and address of bankers

Name and address of two trade references

Estimated monthly credit

Would you be willing to accept
a pro-forma invoice if the credit
assessment is not available
immediately?

Are you aware of our
terms and conditions
of supply?

For office use only	
Credit sanction	
Credit limit	
Account Number	

Letter following up bank reference

Timpsons Furniture Ltd
6 Warburton Avenue
Barnet
Hertfordshire
EN7 4RF

Telephone: 000000
Telex: 000000
Fax: 000000

The Manager,
Midlays Bank Ltd
6 Frost Street
Barnet
Herts
EN13 4DC

10 March 19____

Dear Sir,

We have received an order from a new customer, Messrs Barker and Growler of 7 Highfield Street, Worcester, WR5 6TJ for goods amounting to £000000.

Messrs Barker and Growler inform us that their bankers are National Southminster, 8 Paragon Parade, Worcester, WR6 7YH. We would be grateful if you could make enquiries on our behalf.

Yours faithfully,

P. Underwood
Director

When your bankers reply they will not go into detail but will simply let you know whether your prospective customer's bankers consider them safe for the amount of credit you propose to allow them. If they do not consider the prospective customer is safe for the amount mentioned they may write saying they are "unable to give any information" about the customer, or that they consider the customer would be "over-extended" by being allowed this much credit.

Letter following up trade reference

When following up the trade references supplied by a prospective customer, you would normally enclose a stamped addressed envelope with your request for information.

Timpsons Furniture Ltd
6 Warburton Avenue
Barnet
Hertfordshire
EN7 4RF

Telephone: 000000
Telex: 000000
Fax: 000000

The Manager,
Crawfords Ltd
7 Heathfield Park
London SW19 8FD

10th March 19___

Dear Sir,

Mr James Scottie, Managing Director of Barker and Growler, Worcester, tells us that he regularly transacts business with you. He now wishes to place an order with us for goods amounting to around £000000. We would be very grateful if you would let us know whether you consider Barker and Growler credit-worthy for this amount.

We enclose a stamped addressed envelope for your reply.

Yours faithfully,

P. Underwood
Director

Enc.

Letter replying to above (1)

Crawfords Ltd
7 Heathfield Park
London
SW19 8FD

PRIVATE AND CONFIDENTIAL

P. Underwood Esq
Timpsons Furniture Ltd
6 Warburton Avenue
Barnet
Hertfordshire
EN7 4RF

14th March 19___

Dear Mr Underwood,

I reply to your letter of 10th March 19___.
Messrs Barker and Growler have an account with us.
They place large orders with us on a regular basis and
have always settled their account promptly.
We consider them to be an extremely reliable
organization.

Naturally, this information is given without
responsibility.

Yours sincerely

D. G. Arnott
Director

Letter replying to above (2)

Crawfords Ltd
7 Heathfield Park
London
SW19 8FD

Your ref:
Our ref: DGA/LWB

<u>PRIVATE AND CONFIDENTIAL</u>

P. Underwood Esq
Timpsons Furniture Ltd
6 Warburton Avenue
Barnet
Hertfordshire
EN7 4RF

14th March 19__

Dear Mr Underwood

<u>Messrs Barker and Growler Ltd, Worcester</u>

Thank you for your letter of 10th March 19__. We have only had two fairly small orders from this firm and so are unable to give you a reference. We found them rather slow at settling their account.

This information is given without responsibility.

Yours sincerely

D. G. Arnott
Director

Bills of Exchange

Though they are less used than formerly, Bills of Exchange are still a convenient method of settling an account in international trade. However the Bill of Exchange has almost disappeared from the home trade. A Bill of Exchange is an order sent by the suppliers of the goods which requires the firm to whom it is addressed to pay a sum of money, either on demand or at a future date. (It can be made payable at sight or at a certain number of days after sight, for example 60 days after sight.)

The person who is sent the Bill of Exchange (the "drawee") must accept the Bill by signing his name across the front of it. This usually takes the form of "Accepted payable at . . ." with the drawee's signature and date, though the signature alone is sufficient.

A Documentary Bill of Exchange guarantees payment. The Bill, together with the shipping documents (the Bill of Lading), insurance policy and the invoice for the goods exported, is given to a bank, and the bank's agent abroad will hand the documents over to the consignee only when he has paid the Bill of Exchange. The bank will often make an advance to the exporter, using the goods as security. A Letter of Hypothecation is a letter allowing a bank that has advanced money on a Documentary Bill of Exchange to sell the goods if the Bill were to be dishonoured. If an export company obtains advances on a regular basis they will often sign a general letter of hypothecation, which will cover future transactions.

Example of a Bill of Exchange

London 5th March 19___   £9,000

At sixty days after Sight Pay to our Order the
    Sum Nine Thousand Pounds Sterling

Value received

To: Etablissements Chat
Coucy-le-Chateau
02380 Aisne
France

                    Signed:
                    Dover Shirt Co. Ltd, Dover

Letter of Credit

Another method of payment is by Letter of Credit. This
is a letter addressed by a banker to a correspondent in
another country asking the correspondent to advance
money to the organization named as the beneficiary
against the credit of the bank sending the letter. An
irrevocable Letter of Credit cannot be cancelled so the
sellers of the goods can be sure they will receive the
money. This method of payment is often used when a
firm is dealing with an unknown customer.

5 Letters in connection with sales

Writing sales letters

A sales letter should be simple, but well-written and carefully planned. It must be both persuasive and friendly.

As in all kinds of writing, it will help you if you think about the person or type of person you are writing to. Unless you can seize the attention of your reader immediately he or she may throw your letter away without reading it, so start your letter by letting your reader know you understand his or her needs. Show that it is in their interests to finish reading your letter. For example:

"As an employer, you will naturally expect your key staff to..."

"Were you aware that there is one insurance company that offers advice and preferential terms exclusively to civil servants and their families?"

Once you have gained the reader's attention you have got to keep him reading. Everyone likes to learn something new, so try to make your letter informative and tell the recipients something they did not know before. If your letter contains lots of useful advice people will certainly read it. Back up what you are saying by explaining why your product or services will be of benefit to your reader. Describe the main advantages of your product – why is it better than the product your reader is using now?

In order to keep people reading your letter word it carefully so that each paragraph leads naturally into the next one. You could end a paragraph with a question so that the recipient will carry on reading to find out the answer. Or you may find it useful to end a paragraph with a phrase like "let me show you what I mean". Use short words and vary the length of your paragraphs and sentences. The length of the whole letter will depend on what you have to say and to whom you are writing. Don't make any letter longer than you need to. Short letters are generally best when you are replying to a general enquiry and longer letters work well when written to people in their own homes.

Lay out your letter using indented paragraphs and numbered points. Have the letter produced in a typeface that is as much like typewriter type as possible, so it will look like an individually typed letter. Do not have letters printed in any other sort of typeface or they will *look* like circulars. Try to make the letter easy on the eye, using capital letters, underlining and perhaps the use of a second colour where it will help.

If you are writing a letter of one page only, aim to have three or four paragraphs, each of a different length. If you are writing a longer letter you will have to use a few "tricks of the trade" to make sure people read on. Try finishing a page half way through an important sentence, so that people will be sure to carry on reading. People usually look at the end of a letter before reading it, to see who it comes from. If you use a postscript and make an important sales point in it they will read that too. You could consider having the postscript in simulated handwriting.

The final paragraph should invite action such as "just phone us for a quotation", "why not return the card now, whilst this offer is still fresh in your mind?"

Each paragraph in the letter should contain one main idea only.

As with circular letters (see page 69), a more professional effect can be created, as well as valuable time saved, by word processing standard sales letters and mailing lists. Each client will receive an individually addressed and printed letter, and even particular amendments and alterations can be incorporated within such standard letters quickly and easily.

Sales letter (1)

Decora Continental Kitchens
9 Bakers Row
Warlingham
Surrey CR3 5LA
Tel: 00000

Dear ...

Thank you for your enquiry. I have pleasure in enclosing your free Continental Kitchen brochure.

As you will see, Decora Kitchens are available in a wide range of exciting colours and designs. Though superbly made by craftsmen using the finest materials, Decora kitchens are surprisingly reasonable in price.

However we feel one of the most important aspects of Decora Kitchens is that we as manufacturers help you plan your own unique kitchen, quote you a total price and once this is agreed our highly skilled team install your kitchen quickly, cleanly and efficiently at no extra cost.

Whatever the size and shape of your present kitchen and whatever problems you think you may have, our consultant will be happy to give you advice and plan your kitchen free of charge as well as providing a quotation.

We have asked our consultant, Mr. D. Corator, to visit you when he is next in your area, which will place you under no obligation as his services are absolutely free.

Yours sincerely

Jane Grant
Managing Director

Sales letter (2)

Dear Sir,

Here is your last chance...

to secure completely free and without any obligation, an attractive imitation leather document wallet. A valuable gift you will use all the time.

Inside your free wallet, you will find a real leather-bound diary, together with a few samples of our extensive range of high quality stationery and our new brochures. Our price list will show you how competitive we are, but what you won't find out, till you try us, is that we also have a very speedy delivery service. Nor will you know that our dependable advisory team are here to help you with any problems. We've got fifty years experience in this field!

Order your free document wallet, real leather-bound diary and stationery samples today – just fill out and return the enclosed card now.

Yours faithfully

P.S. There is another gift for you when you place your first stationery order!

Letter of enquiry (1)

Weston Sewing Machines Ltd
Queen Mary's Avenue
Epworth
Near Doncaster
S Yorks DN8 5TG

Ridings & Cooper Ltd
5 Castleton Street
Crewe
Cheshire
CW2 7BR

20 March 19___

Dear Sirs

We are interested in your Johnson 850 Knitting Machines and would be grateful if you would send us your catalogue. Please state your best trade prices and earliest delivery date.

Yours faithfully

R. P. Morley
Sales Manager

Letter replying to above

Ridings & Cooper Ltd
5 Castleton Street
Crewe
Cheshire CW2 7ER

Weston Sewing Machines Ltd
Queen Mary's Avenue
Epworth
S. Yorks DN8 5TG

24th March 19__

Dear Sirs

We were delighted to receive your enquiry about the
Johnson 850 Knitting Machine and are sending you a
copy of our latest fully illustrated catalogue and price
list.

We have good supplies of most of the sewing and
knitting machines in the catalogue and can supply
them within two weeks of receiving an order.

Of course, the best way to examine the Johnson 850 is
to see the machine working, and our representative for
your area, Mr F. Sanders, would be happy to call on
you and demonstrate the machine. We have asked him
to telephone you within the next few days to arrange
an appointment.

We are sure you will be delighted with the Johnson
machine and look forward to the pleasure of doing
business with you.

Yours faithfully
for RIDINGS & COOPER

Stanley Bagshot

Letter of enquiry (2)

Mackay and Parrish Ltd
12 Upper Parade
Ashtead
Surrey
KT22 3AG

Plastart Ltd
24 Regency Row
London
E5 9LR

28th October 19__

Dear Sirs

We understand that you are manufacturers of carrier
bags and would be grateful if you would send us
samples of the various qualities, styles and sizes and
let us have an estimate of the costs of printing 50,000
bags on both sides in one colour only from artwork
supplied.

Would you please also give us an indication of the
delivery time from receipt of artwork.

Yours faithfully

G. Green

Placing an order or asking for a quotation

Even if you are placing an order or asking a supplier for a quotation you should not forget that your letter must help to foster a good business relationship and that it should be persuasive. What you want from your supplier is a fair price, perhaps even a reduction in price, a quality product, prompt delivery and good after-sales service.

To get these things you must get your supplier to cooperate with you. Never be aggressive or impolite. This attitude might get you a cheaper price or faster delivery once, but it will make your working relationship much more strained in the future. Rather, ask for the supplier's help and try to make helpful suggestions to him. When asking for a quotation get his ideas on the cheapest and best way of planning the job. Make sure your order, or request for a quotation is clear and that it includes all the relevant facts. When getting a quotation from several suppliers – and you should of course do this – get them all to quote on the same basis, otherwise you will not be able to compare prices accurately. You will probably find it useful to give each of them a job specification in writing.

Incidentally, a quotation is a firm figure whereas an estimate is a general forecast of what the cost are likely to be.

Placing an order

Most commercial firms produce their own standardized order forms, most of the information being printed and the relevant details typed as required. The terms and conditions are often printed on the reverse side of the order form. Such order forms are often produced in pads with serially-numbered pages.

Orders placed by letter should give full details, referring to the supplier's quotation or quoting the serial or catalogue number of the goods ordered where applicable. Make sure that directions for forwarding are given, that is, delivery date, delivery address (and how the items should be packed and who they should be addressed to), method of transport and whether carriage paid or carriage forward.

Confirm the price and the agreed terms of payment, stating any discount which has been given. If you place an order over the telephone, confirm it in writing, making it clear that the order is a confirmation of your telephoned order and not another order for the same type of goods.

Letter placing order

Our Order No. 89/4575

Jones and Cooper Ltd
Marlborough Road
Leicester
Leicestershire
LE5 3AT

19th March 19__

J. Brooks Esq
Sales Manager
The Midland Wine Shippers Ltd
Bentley Road
Birmingham B4 5TG

Dear Mr Brooks

Please supply the following cases of wine to our shop at 3 Burton Lane, Leicester, Carriage Paid:

Quantity	Description
100 cases	Westfield Character Vintage Port
200 cases	St Louis French White Table Wine
250 cases	St Louis French Red Table Wine
50 cases	Franco Bollo Frascati
25 cases	von Bilderling Liebfraumilch 1978

In accordance with your quotation date 14th March 19__, reference Sales/DW. Prices to include delivery.
Delivery: one week from receipt of order.
Packages: charged extra but credited in full on return.
Terms: 2½% cash discount.

Yours sincerely

J. W. Maynard

Acknowledgement of order

Some order forms are designed so that there is a per-
forated acknowledgement slip at the bottom which can
be signed by the supplier and returned. Sometimes
order forms are supplied in pads with an extra copy to
be sent to the supplier, who signs and returns it.
Where no such arrangement exists, it is still essential
to acknowledge all orders received, otherwise there
might be considerable delay should the order form go
astray.

When you receive a first order from a new customer,
you will create goodwill if you send a letter acknowledging the order and welcoming the firm as your
customer.

Letter acknowledging order (1)

Midland Wine Shippers Ltd
Bentley Road
Our ref: Sales/DW   Birmingham B4 5TG

Your ref: Order 89/4575

For the attention of J. W. Maynard

Jones and Cooper Ltd
Marlborough Road
Leicester
Leicestershire
LE5 3AT

21st March 19

Dear Sirs,

We are writing to thank you very much for your
order of 19th October and to welcome you as one of our
customers.

We can supply from stock all the wines ordered and our van will deliver them to you on Friday 27th March. We feel certain all these lines will sell extremely well in your area. They represent particularly good value for money and we can only offer them at such keen prices because we ship these wines ourselves.

You may be interested to know that we also stock some fine sherries and ports at various prices. Our range is more fully described in the enclosed price list and catalogue.

We hope that our handling of this order will lead to more business between us and we look forward to establishing a close business relationship

Yours faithfully
for MIDLAND WINE SHIPPERS LTD.

J. Wibley

Enc.

Letter acknowledging order (2)

Bannister and Hyde Ltd
(Display Equipment)
Sparkbrook Lane
Birmingham B6 5JJ

Ref: PJW/859

8th January 19__

J. Parker Esq
Midland Packaging Co
7 Weston Place
Birmingham B4 3HB

Dear Mr Parker

Your order number 7046/81

I would like to thank you for your recent order for 100 leaflet dispensers in brown plastic.

Your order is scheduled for dispatch during the week commencing 19th May. If your goods have not arrived within seventeen days of that date please notify us immediately so we can investigate the matter with the road transport company.

As you are in this area, you may prefer to collect your order yourselves. If so please telephone our Dispatch Department on Birmingham 00000. It would help if you could quote our reference to them.

Please check that your order is undamaged as we cannot accept claims for damaged stock after 28 days.

I do hope the leaflet dispensers will meet with your approval and that they will give you every satisfaction.

Yours truly

C. Bush
Sales Manager

Giving quotations

A quotation should start by thanking the potential customers for their enquiry. It should be clearly set out and should state exactly what the quoted prices cover, for example, packing individually, packing in bulk, delivery to one address, insurance. An undertaking should be given as to the date of delivery. Because the price of raw materials is subject to inflation it is important to state the period for which the quotation will remain valid. A quotation may also state the terms of payment and whether a discount is given for prompt or cash payment or payment in advance.

Letter of quotation

Rossiter Ltd
294 Brook Road
Sheffield
South Yorkshire
S10 5DX

B. Tillotson Esq
Groves & Jameson Ltd
12 Mill Way
Sheffield
South Yorkshire
S3 4BN

11th November 19__

Dear Mr Tillotson

Thank you for your enquiry of 8th November about 'Merman' Bathrooms. I have today sent you a copy of our colour catalogue in which you will see our range of sanitary ware and bathroom accessories, and I am pleased to quote for a number of sample items as follows:

	White	Coloured
Acrylic Bath	£73.70	£84.70
Basin	15.60	16.45
Pedestal	10.80	11.40
Cistern	34.55	36.40
Pan	32.05	33.65
Seat	12.40	13.05

The prices are exclusive of VAT but include delivery to your warehouse and are valid for four weeks from the date of this letter.

'Merman' bathroom equipment has an unrivalled reputation for high quality and design at very keen prices. We hold stocks of the 'Merman' range in twelve attractive shades, including the new 'Wild Orchid' and 'Sorrento', and we can deliver within two weeks of receiving an order.

The prices quoted are for orders of invoice value £1000. For larger orders we offer an extra 5% discount. Our terms of payment are 2½% per month.

We are sure you will find our prices satisfactory and look forward to hearing from you.

Yours sincerely

G. V. Booker

Example of standard quotation form

<u>QUOTATION</u>   Number: 53900

STARLET COSMETICS LIMITED
133/135 Blenheim Green,
Coventry CV2 1GH

Tel: Coventry 00000   5th March 19__

Blondefair Ltd
Earls Barton
Northampton
NN7 6HJ

Re: Your enquiry No. 58 dated 27th February 19__

Catalogue Reference	Quantity	Description	Price per doz.
1598/AB	10 doz.	'Juliana' Make-up Remover	£00.00
1989/5/A	5 doz.	'Juliana' Mascara	£00.00
0045/Z	15 doz.	Oatmeal Face Pack	£00.00
0046/Z	15 doz.	Lemon & Honey Face Pack	£00.00
67/E/S	10 doz.	Assorted Eye-shadows	£00.00
2356	5 doz.	'Rosa' Lipsticks	£00.00

Plus VAT at 00%
Delivery: by carrier within 7 days of receipt of order.
20% Trade Discount from orders over £000 before
VAT.
2½% cash discount for payment within 15 days of date
of invoice.
Carriage paid to your premises.

Using standard form letters

Most firms use 'standard form letters', as quite a large proportion of their correspondence is repetitious in that they are sending the same information to different people. They therefore draft letters with a series of sentences and paragraphs that are suitable for the same situation: for example, acknowledgement of enquiries and orders, forwarding price lists or catalogues, expected delivery dates, debt collection letters, applications for employment, to mention but a few.

Setting up a standard form letter system

Standard form letters will reduce the costs of correspondence and assist in the speedy answering of routine enquiries, saving both the dictator's and the typist's time. To set up a form letter system you obviously need to analyse what sort of routine letters are sent out frequently. So for a few weeks make extra copies of all your outgoing correspondence. At the end of the period sort your correspondence by subject matter to determine the types of letter sent out most often and the most frequently used phrases and paragraphs. Choose the best example of each, improving on it if possible. Make sure it is neither officious nor pompous.

It is, of course, absolutely essential that the person who drafts a standard form letter or paragraph makes it as accurate, unambiguous and readable as possible, because otherwise it will confuse not only one correspondent but many, and the whole purpose of preparing a standard form draft in the first place will be undermined.

Conditions change and so form letters quickly become out of date. You should set up a new system every twelve months or so.

The master copies of each standard form letter should be placed in a loose-leaf folder, called a Form Book. They should be numbered and classified or indexed. You will need at least two identical copies of the Form Book, one for the dictator and one for the typist.

The person dictating tells the typist to use 'standard' numbered paragraphs from the Form Book. An extra dictated paragraph can be added to cover a point not touched on by any of the standard paragraphs in the Form Book. One criticism of form letters is that they are not sympathetic to individual cases and the addition of a specially dictated paragraph can help to overcome this. Properly used, the form letter system will ensure that only carefully prepared and accurate letters are sent out. Composite letters which are produced from standard paragraphs need not be stilted. The typist can be asked to alter the wording slightly so that the transition from one paragraph to another will run smoothly.

Printed letters are not given as much attention by their recipients as personally typed ones so the majority of firms prefer not to print or duplicate standard form letters but to have them typed out when needed.

Below are examples of the sort of phrases you would expect to find in a Form Book:

1 Thank you for your letter of ...
2 Thank you for your enquiry of ...
3 Thank you for your order no. ..., which we received today.
4 Since we know that you are the buyers of ..., we enclose our price list which gives full particulars, and are also sending you separately samples of our principal types/qualities/ranges ...
5 As this is the first order which you have sent to us,

we should be pleased if, in accordance with our firm's practice, you would send us the names and addresses of two firms with which you have regularly done business.

6 We can deliver the goods within ... weeks from the date of your order.

7 We apologise for our delay in replying to your letter of ... but this was caused ...

8 Would you please let us know what the latest position is on this order. We should be most grateful if you could improve upon the delivery time shown on the order sheet.

9 Our sales representative, Mr/Mrs/Ms ..., will call at your office on ... at ... to give you any further information you need.

You might dictate two letters as follows:

Letter No. 1. To D. Husband & Sons Ltd.
    Paragraph 3: S. 134
    Paragraph 5 two – satisfactory references

Letter No. 2 – sent to suppliers because of lack of materials urgently required.
To The Grayshield Manufacturing Co., Ltd.
    Paragraph 8: Order No. B. 163.

Example of a standard form letter

CREASE AND PENDRIGH
214-220 Sunset Boulevard
Cowplain, Hampshire
PO6 2LR
8th July 19__

Our ref: UR80

Mr Edward Cray,
25 Beau Rivage Crescent,
Canvey Island,
Essex SO4 1LT

Dear Sir,

Thank you for your letter of 7th July.

It is our usual practice to supply new customers with our goods together with an invoice for payment within one month of the date of the invoice in the first instance. For subsequent orders we will extend the time for payment to three months.

We hope you will use our services and are sending you separately by parcel post samples of our different qualities, together with our price lists.

We shall deal with your orders promptly.

Yours faithfully,

CREASE AND PENDRIGH.

Using printed forms

Sometimes printed forms can be used to cut down routine internal and external correspondence. Much standard material can be printed on the form, which cuts down writing and helps to ensure that all relevant information will be included. Forms should be printed on a standard size of paper to fit existing filing systems and so they will fit a standard envelope if they are to be mailed. If you are sending out quantities of forms, consider the weight of the paper they are printed on, which can add to your postage costs. Different colours of paper can help recognition and simplify filing.

The design of a form should be as simple as possible. Care should be taken in wording them so they do not go out of date quickly. Make sure enough space is left on the form to include all the necessary information. Before you have the blank forms duplicated or printed, take a copy of the artwork or the typed master form and fill it out. In this way you will be able to satisfy yourself that enough room has been left.

Incidentally, when planning a new form, avoid the wording 'Christian name' – there are a lot of people in this country who are not Christians, and you would not wish to offend them; use 'first name' or 'given name' instead.

Example of a printed form

T. E. Barnes Ltd
78 Willan Road
Liverpool L6 5HN

Our ref.

(Leave (i.e. turn up) 11 or 12 single-line spaces)

For the attention of
(Leave (i.e. turn up) 4 single-line spaces)

Dear Sirs,

Thank you for your order number *(leave 10 blank spaces)*
dated *(leave 16 blank spaces)*. We will be able to
deliver the order in *(leave 4 blank spaces)* weeks.

Yours faithfully,

T. E. BARNES LTD.

6 Complaints

Making complaints

If you have to make a complaint, do so tactfully and courteously. There are some people who think – quite wrongly – that because someone has made a mistake they are entitled to be disgruntled, and they therefore write sarcastic letters of complaint. In such circumstances, sarcasm and anger, although possibly therapeutic to the writer, may only antagonize the recipient and could destroy a good business relationship which has lasted for several years.

It is far better to assume that, if someone has made a mistake, the firm whose employee was responsible is likely to be more worried than the person making the complaint, that is, if the firm is proud of its reputation. Only if the person complaining does not receive a full and frank explanation of what went wrong is he wise to come back in a more aggressive manner.

Your first letter should always be to the person directly responsible for sorting out your problems. If that does not work you can write to his or her superior or to the Managing Director or other executive, by name if possible. Write a firm but polite letter, so that you will get the Managing Director's sympathy. State the facts of your case clearly in a brief letter, quoting dates, names and events. Do not merely say what is wrong – tell your correspondent exactly how he can put the matter right. In your final paragraph express confidence that the problem will be solved quickly and amicably.

Answering complaints

You may not exactly enjoy receiving a letter of complaint but you should still welcome the letter. Why?

There are good reasons. First of all it may show you that something has gone wrong, or seems to have gone wrong, inside your organization, and give you the chance to put matters right. Secondly, it is better to get a complaint from a customer yourself than to learn about the complaint at third hand – after your customer has left you for a rival supplier and told all and sundry how badly you have treated him. Thirdly, a complaint will provide you with an excellent opportunity to improve your organization's goodwill, by answering in a helpful manner.

Make it known to all your customers that you want to know about any complaints they may have at any time. Make sure they realize they can always turn to you if they think something has gone wrong with your products or services.

Never reject a complaint – you may lose not only the customer in question but other customers or potential customers who hear about the complaint. Don't forget that someone who feels he or she has been unfairly treated is bound to tell other people their sad story. In the same way, if you deal correctly with the complaint you may even win customers.

Delays in dealing with complaints are obvious sources of fresh annoyance. Answer every complaint straight away. If the matter needs investigation, send a short note or postcard acknowledging receipt of the letter and then reply fully as soon as you can. Do not be critical nor offhand. Never argue, but take the attitude that your correspondent is trying to help you. If the complaint is justified admit readily that you are at fault, express your regret and apologize for any trouble caused (though if you suspect a law suit may follow, beware), explain the reason why things went wrong simply and honestly and undertake to put the matter right. If necessary you should also offer to pay for any indirect costs that may have been caused by your company's error. Don't forget to check and make sure that the same sort of mistake can never happen again!

Justified complaints are really the easiest ones to deal with. All you have to do is apologize and put things right. The matter is more difficult if the complaint is unjustified, and even more tact is required. If the complaint is an unreasonable one, don't be tempted to rebuff your correspondent. Explain the situation in a way that does not cause offence – don't set out to prove to your customer that he or she is in the wrong. Explain the situation in a way that does not cause offence, remembering that people are often far from calm when they make a complaint and may not react rationally to what they sense to be a dismissive attitude on the part of the organization they are complaining to.

If you can offer constructive suggestions as to how the person or organization making the complaint can avoid similar trouble in future, do so. Try to convince them that you are treating them fairly and that your rejection of their complaint does not mean you do not care about them or that you underestimate their importance. Explain the position in detail and establish that the fault cannot have been yours. However, do not say the fault was on the other side. It may well have been, of course, but let the person who made the complaint deduce this for himself.

If you are helpful when dealing with a complaint which may not be justified this does not imply that you accept the blame.

Of course, there may be times when you feel it is worth accepting at least part of the blame, even when it is unjustified, in order to keep a valued customer happy. You may find that the compensation you pay will be more than offset in increased orders in the future.

Letter of complaint (1)

M. Bannister and Co. Ltd.,
Bannister Works,
Garrick Lane,
East Finchley,
London, N2 1HC

Ref: HGPT/JM   16th June 19__

J. Rossiter Esq
Lamptons Ltd
Lamptons Industrial Estate
Chiswick
London W4 1BL

Dear Sirs,

<u>Our order No. P439</u>

We understand from our foreman who inspected the batch of blankets which we received from you last week that they were of a much poorer quality than your usual supply.

We are returning one of these blankets together with one from a previous order so that you may compare. The latest batch is a shade darker in colour as well as being inferior in quality.

Would you please let us have your report as soon as possible.

Yours faithfully,
for M. Bannister and Co. Ltd.

D. Ingram

Letter replying to above

Lamptons Ltd
Lamptons Industrial Estate
Your ref: HGPT/JM   Chiswick
London
Our ref: BVL/JG   W4 1BL

M. Bannister and Co. Ltd.,
Bannister Works,
Garrick Lane,
East Finchley,
London,
N2 1HC

18th June 19___

Dear Sirs,

<u>Your order No. P 439</u>

We are very sorry to learn from your letter of 16th
June that you are not satisfied with the batch of
blankets we sent you on 10th June. We are very
concerned but nevertheless pleased that you have
raised this matter with us.

As you know, we have been stocking these particular
blankets for some years now. They are very long-
lasting and represent good value for money and it is
very unfortunate that the last batch did not come up to
the usual high quality and that the dye used appears to
be of a different shade.

We have taken the matter up with the manufacturers
and are sure that in future they will supply only
blankets of top quality.

We are certain you will wish to continue stocking
these blankets, which are such good sellers, and in the

circumstances suggest that we replace this batch of blankets and offer you an extra 5% discount on the order as a gesture of goodwill.

Our van will be in your area next Friday and can deliver the replacement blankets and collect the faulty ones then.

Meanwhile please accept our apologies for the inconvenience you have been caused.

Yours faithfully,

J. Rossiter
Manager

Letter of complaint (2)

STAN RAE & SONS LTD
Sunray House
Oxford OX3 1QQ

18th June 19___

Ref: LR/MKB

Slipshod and Shoddy Ltd.,
Painters and Decorators,
Scandal House
1 Bodger Road
Oxford OX3 1LM

Dear Sirs,

After your workmen left one of our company's houses, Raewood House, Mangetout Road, Oxford, last Friday, one of our directors, Mr Bernard Rae, called to inspect the premises to complete the final arrangements for our new works manager to occupy them at the end of the month. He noticed that your workmen had not carried out the necessary work as satisfactorily as your firm have done when you have worked for us in the past.

Mr Rae listed the following:

(1) The window frames in the sitting-room have been completely missed.
(2) Brush marks are clearly visible in the bathroom and there are finger marks on one wall.
(3) The finish of the ceiling in the larger bedroom is unsatisfactory.

Although you have handled several contracts for us in recent years, this is the first time we have had reason to be dissatisfied. Would you therefore please send your foreman round to the house to see the work for himself and to give instructions to ensure that your workmen finish the work to our satisfaction by the end of next week at the latest.

Yours faithfully
for STAN RAE & SONS LTD.

Leslie Robertson

Letter of complaint (3)

D. DANN & SONS,
Hartley Chambers,
Bolton,
BO3 1LT

5th June 19___

Ref: SC/VR

The Barnett Paint Co. Ltd.,
Weston Street,
WORCESTER,
WO5 3XY

Dear Sirs,

Order No. 150

You will be sorry to learn that the paint which you delivered to us by carrier yesterday has been badly damaged in transit.

When we unpacked it, we discovered that the tins of powder blue paint had been so severely crushed and broken that the contents of four one-gallon tins had completely escaped into the packing material and have therefore become unfit for use.

We notified the carriers and an officer in their Goods Department immediately called here to inspect the damaged tins. He told us that, while his firm would be prepared to meet a claim for the loss involved, he was of the opinion that the tin containers had been too thin for the paint to be transported safely and that, moreover, the cases used were insufficiently soundly constructed to protect the tins. He suggested that thicker wood should have been used.

We should be grateful if you would send us four more one-gallon tins of powder blue paint to replace those which were damaged and if you would make sure that they arrive safely.

Yours faithfully,

D. DANN & SONS

Letter replying to above

The Barnett Paint Co. Ltd.,
Weston Street,
Worcester,
WO5 3XY

Your ref: SC/VB   7th June 19___

D. Dann & Sons,
Hartley Chambers,
Bolton, BO3 1LT

Dear Sirs,

<u>Your order No. 150</u>

Thank you for your letter of 5th June. We were very sorry to hear of the damage to the consignment of paint which we delivered under the above order.

This is the first complaint of this nature that we have received, and we are rather surprised to hear that the damage may have been attributed in part to the structure of the tin containers and in part to inadequate packing. In fact, we use the same tin containers for shipments abroad, though, of course, more substantial packing is essential to meet export requirements. However our packaging department will be giving this matter serious attention and carrying out suitable tests, so that if necessary we can take steps to prevent any more problems.

As requested, we have sent you today a further four one-gallon tins of the paint you require in case No. G.P. 285 under Advice Note No. 346, and hope you will receive these in good condition.

We apologize for any convenience which you have been caused.

Yours faithfully,

THE BARNETT PAINT CO. LTD.

Letter of complaint (4)

Tate and Freeman Ltd
23 Wyatt Road
BIRMINGHAM
B24 5RL

7th September 19__

Martin Parker & Sons Ltd
146 Lower Street
Aberdeen
AB3 4TH

Dear Sirs

On checking your invoice No. 786/F, we find that you
have charged the full list-price for items 5, 7 and 14.
We are sure this must be a mistake because in the past
you have charged us your wholesale rates.
Please check this in your records and then send us
either a new invoice or a credit note.

Yours faithfully

S. TATE

Replying to above

This is a simple letter to reply to. If a mistake has been made write apologizing and enclosing the credit note they have requested.

Letter of complaint (5)

Saville's Chemists
1 Park Road
Cambridge CB4 3AD

4th May 19__

Suntan Sunglasses Ltd
7 Lower Road
Crawley
West Sussex
RH11 7SX

Dear Sirs,

<u>Our order No. B 45/82</u>

We have still not received six boxes of the sunglasses we ordered from you two months ago. I am sure your firm is as keen as we are to ensure that these sunglasses are in the shops by the beginning of the holiday period, the peak time for sales. Can you therefore please let us know when we may expect delivery of the sunglasses.

Yours faithfully,

P. Saville

The chemist need never have written the letter above if his suppliers had kept him fully informed. However, the letter below should restore good relations.

Letter replying to above

Suntan Sunglasses Ltd
7 Lower Road
Crawley
West Sussex
RH11 7SX

Saville's Chemists Ltd
1 Park Road
Cambridge
CB4 3AD

6th May 19___

Dear Sirs,

Your order B. 45/82

Thank you for your letter of 4th May about the sunglasses you have ordered. I am very sorry to say there have been a number of problems with the manufacturer of these sunglasses and at the moment we are unable to supply your order. Of course we are very anxious to have the sunglasses on the market for the summer season and are doing everything we can to obtain supplies of them as quickly as possible. Nevertheless we will fully understand it if you feel compelled to cancel your order. May we suggest you wait until the end of May and we will let you know the position then. In the meantime we will continue to put pressure on the manufacturers.

Yours faithfully,

Sales Director

7 Other written communications

The Memorandum

The inter-office or internal memorandum is a method of sending written information to a member of the same organization. Some companies use pre-printed forms for internal communication, and in others the information is typed on a sheet of plain paper. Memoranda are often handwritten. Unlike a letter a memorandum needs neither an inside name and address, salutation nor complimentary close. Usually the person originating the memorandum, or 'memo' will sign or initial it.

Example of memorandum (1)

MEMORANDUM

TO: DATE:
    Miss M Jones   12 November 19__
    Publicity Manager

FROM: REFERENCE:
    John Wilson   JW/ASKN
    Sales Director

                             SUBJECT:
                                 Spring Sales
                                 Conference

This is to let you know that the Spring Sales
Conference will be held on 3rd, 4th and
5th January at the Berkeley Hotel,
Livermore Street, Blackthorn.
Perhaps you would me know whether there are
any items you wish to include on the Agenda.

Example of memorandum (2)

To: Mr B. Davies
     Production Controller

From: B. A. Johnson
     Managing Director

28th October 19__

BAJ/BVL

<u>PRIVATE</u>

John Baker of Cartwright and Summers telephoned me today and told me that he had not had any reply to an urgent letter they wrote you two weeks ago. I of course assured them that it is most unusual for anyone in this Company not to answer their correspondence promptly and have told them you will come back to them and let them know what happened.

I assume that either their letter or your reply to it has gone astray in the post and if this is the case no doubt you will get in contact with them straight away. If you have received their letter and have not yet replied to it, please do so immediately, apologizing for the delay, and at the same time let me know what happened.

Minutes of meetings

The Minutes of a meeting are a summary, written in the third person, of what was done and said at a meeting.

Usually presented in the order of the Agenda, Minutes state the date and place where the meeting was held, the names and, where relevant titles, of those present, the business discussed and the decisions reached. Minutes provide not only an authentic record of what happened at the meeting but also serve to provide information for people who did not attend.

The person who takes the Minutes, usually the Secretary, should ensure that though the Minutes are as brief as possible, they are an accurate record of the meeting. It is a good idea to write up the Minutes as soon as possible after a meeting, while the meeting is fresh in the memory. Minutes from the previous meeting are read at the next and signed by the Chairman as being a true record of the meeting. It is also common for those Minutes to be circulated before a meeting and then to be "taken as read".

Written reports

Written reports are a very important means of transmitting and receiving information. They must be presented in a lively, clear, orderly way. The tone of a report is usually more formal than that of a business letter and it is normally written in the third person.

One of the main problems to overcome is the fact that the person writing the report knows so much about his subject that he writes in too technical language. He may include too much information, or he might omit steps in his argument, because to him they seem obvious, and fail to make the significance of his investigations clear to the reader.

Before writing anything, you should decide who your readers will be. Do they already know something about the subject and can you omit this information from your report? Why is the report necessary – what background information, ideas, facts, conclusions and recommendations should be included? Keep these points in mind whilst collecting your material and writing the report.

Collecting and assembling relevent information is just as important as the actual writing of the report. You may find it helpful to set up a card index system, or to use a loose-leaf folder with a separate sheet of paper for each section of your proposed report. This will enable you to rearrange the sections and put them into a logical sequence, either in order of their importance or in chronological order.

Layout of reports

The person typing a report should be instructed to lay out each page so it is attractive and easy to read.

Wide margins should be provided on both sides of the paper. The left-hand margin ensures that there is room to bind the report without losing some of the text, while the right-hand margin concentrates the text into a narrow column, making it much quicker to read. It allows the author of the report to provide marginal references or notes, which are neater and less distracting for the reader than footnotes. The reader of the report can also make comments in the right-hand margin.

The use of underlined headings, capital letters, indented paragraphs and a clear system of numbering the sections will make the report easier to read.

For a full-scale report, a practical way to arrange the information is:

1   **Title and Identification.** A long report normally starts with a separate sheet which forms the front cover, and which bears the title of the report. The title must be self-explanatory so that the report could easily be located if filed away in a library. It should give the name of the person who submitted it and the date the report was made.

2   **Contents Page.** This will help your reader to find at a glance the parts of the report which are relevant to him. Unless your report is very long indeed, you will not need an index if you have provided a well-constructed contents list.

3   **Synopsis of the Work Done, Conclusions and Recommendations.** This will help the person in a hurry, who just wants to know the answer, and will make it easier for people reading the whole report to follow your arguments and assess the relevance of each part of the report. Although the synopsis

comes at the beginning of a report, it cannot, of course be written until after the detailed report, which it summarizes, has been compiled.

4 **Main Body of the Report.** This will contain an introduction, setting out the terms of reference, the work done, the methods of investigation and sources from which the information has been collected as well as the conclusions reached and recommendations for future action.

This will almost certainly be the longest part of the report and so will need dividing into sections. You may wish to put a graph or thumbnail sketch in the right-hand margin, so it will be as near to the relevant text as possible. Otherwise group all this information together in an appendix, giving each diagram an identifying caption.

5 **Glossary of Terms.** Non-specialists who will read your report may need an explanation of the technical terms. If you explain a term the first time it occurs in the report the explanation may not be seen by someone who only wishes to study a certain section of the report, so the explanation would have to be repeated each time the word cropped up, which would certainly annoy the specialists! If there are only one or two technical phrases you might choose to explain them by a note at the beginning of the report.

6 **Acknowledgements.** If you have drawn on material from outside sources, books, articles in journals or reports of investigations carried out by other organizations, you should list your sources.

7 **Specialist Section.** Keep specialist material, which may be of interest to only a few readers, outside the body of the report. Appendices can contain experimental data, statistical information,

156

tables, graphs, diagrams and sketches. The appendices should be titled and listed, A, B, C, etc. or they can be distinguished by the use of different coloured paper.

8 **Distribution List.** It is helpful to readers to know who else has received a copy of a report. They can also see who has not had a copy and arrange for them to receive one if necessary.

Press releases

Editorial publicity in the press and broadcasts is extremely effective. Not only is it a great deal cheaper – though not easier to obtain – than paid advertising, but it is more valuable. The general public is quite rightly sceptical of advertising but will usually believe the editorial columns of their favourite magazine or newspaper. One method of getting items of news to magazines, newspapers, trade journals, radio and television is the press release. Because these media receive large numbers of press releases each day, it is important to write your press release to make it interesting to the readers of the journal you are sending it to, and to send it to the right person on the journal, radio or television station in question.

A press release should be typed and printed or duplicated on one side only of A4 paper. Use double spacing between the lines and extra space between paragraphs. Leave a wide margin on each side of the paper. Do not forget that you are not writing an advertisement – do not mention your company or its products too often. Copy the style of the journals you are aiming at – they almost certainly use short paragraphs, so you should too. Check for typing and spelling errors – if you are mentioning a visiting dignitary, make sure you have their full name (correctly spelled), honours and other relevant information.

Your first paragraph should contain the bare bones of the story, so that it can stand alone and do its job if there is only space for a short mention of your product or services. Subsequent paragraphs will just add more information.

Ideally a Press Release should not exceed one page. But if it does you should indicate at the bottom of the first page that it is continued. A good way of doing this is to put 'More...' on the bottom right-hand corner.

At the bottom of the last page of the press release you should put:

For further information please contact (*name, phone number*)

You must make sure that you, or whoever you have named at the end of the press release, really does have further information!

A quick check-list for press releases

1 Products
What it is
Is it new?
Is it different?
Made of
Made by/designed by
When in the shops/
  which shops
Price

2 People
Full names
Correct spelling
Profession, honours
  etc
Age
Marital status/
  children
Where they live/work
Interest/hobbies

3 Occasions/Events
What
When
Where
Why

**4 Successes/orders/
  deals etc**
What
When
To whom
What's it worth

House magazines and newsletters

These are produced for your staff, customers or share-holders, and obviously they will differ according to which of these readerships they are aimed at. The golden rule is to make them as lively and interesting as possible and to remember that people love reading about themselves and people they know well. It would be worthwhile, incidentally, to send copies of your house magazine to the press; if there is something that interests them they may use it and quote the source.

Advertising

Advertising in general is outside the scope of this book and if you plan to do a large amount of advertising you would be well advised to consult a specialist agency. However for organizations who want to insert an occasional advertisement in a newspaper or journal, a few hints may be helpful: Choose your advertising medium carefully. Is the publication read by the people who will buy your product? Before booking the advertisement think what you have to say. Is the space large enough? You might find it helpful to draw out the shape of the advertisement, so you can see clearly the area you have to fill. Should you book your advertise-ment to appear on a particular day of the week? If so, which day? Should you choose a run-of-paper advertise-ment – that is one which appears wherever the make-up man on the publication decides to put it – or should you pay extra to have it on the letters page, the entertain-ments page or near the recruitment advertisements?

Make your advertisement interesting and informa-tive, look for the main sales point and put it to your potential customers in a way that will prove your offer is worthwhile. You must tell the truth of course. If you are illustrating your advertisement the picture and the headline should work hand in hand with one another.

As when writing a letter, you will find it helps to imagine the person you are appealing to. Try to write your advertisement with a real person in mind. Do not talk down to your prospective customers – nor use technical jargon unless your customer will understand what you mean. It is usually safest to assume that though your customer is intelligent he or she knows nothing about the product or service advertised.

Though perhaps not very original, this format can work very well: at the top of the advertisement should be a headline conveying specific information. Under this place an illustration of your product. Make sure this will reproduce clearly. A very detailed photograph will not reproduce to best advantage in newspapers. Below the illustration should be your copy – this should be easy to read and to understand. First list the principal selling points of your product in bold type and then go on to explain about the product in more detail in a less prominent typeface.

Example of notice convening meeting of creditors

RAMSHACKLE AND TUMBLEDOWN BUILDERS LTD

Notice is hereby given pursuant to section 293 of The Companies Act 1948 that a meeting of the creditors of the above named company will be held at Brockenhurst House, 78 Liverpool Road, Bickley, on Wednesday 3rd September 19___, at 12.15 pm for the purpose mentioned in sections 294 and 295 of The Companies Act 1948.

Dated this 15th day of August 19___

A. TUMBLEDOWN
Director

Example of application for a Justices' On-Licence

To the Clerk to the Licensing Justices for the
Licensing District of South Eastern Division.
To the Chief Officer of Police for the Police Area of the
said District.
To the Proper Officer of the London Borough of _____.
To the Fire Authority of the Greater London Council
and to all whom it may concern.

Take notice that I Michael Thripp of 78 Wellington
Road, Catford, SE6 2AG having for the last six months
carried on the trade or calling of a Restauranteur
intend to apply at the Licensing Sessions to be held at
the Town Hall, Catford, London on the 9th day of
September 19__ at ten o'clock in the forenoon for the
grant to me of a New Justices' On-Licence of the
description of Restaurant Licence authorizing me to
sell intoxicating liquor of all descriptions on the
premises situate at 9 Honeyview Walk, London, SE13
5TJ, a plan of which premises has been deposited with
the Clerk to the Licensing Justices together with this
notice.

Dated the 14th day of August 19__.

Plummers
Authorised Agent on
behalf of the
Applicant

8 Telecommunications – telephone, Telex and telegram

Why telephone?

Letter or telephone call? There is a place for both. Apart from the financial consideration, the telephone is immediate. It provides a direct link and can help to establish a more personal relationship. People respond immediately to the telephone. A letter can be put aside to be answered at a later date but the telephone demands attention. Even if you are in a meeting you probably answer the phone as soon as it rings. When listening to a telephone conversation people also concentrate in the way they may not do when reading a letter. Problems can be discussed and any doubtful points clarified straight away. Confidential matters, which if written down might reach the wrong hands, can be discussed more easily.

A letter, however, provides a written record of a transaction. Though you can plan in advance what you are going to say in a telephone conversation, you will not know how the person receiving the call will react. A letter enables you to think out your argument in advance and state it clearly. If necessary, you can discuss your planned letter with your colleagues and it can be approved by a superior before it is sent.

It is often easier to write a letter if you have something upsetting or embarrassing to say. The telephone is an extremely sensitive reflector of attitude and mood.

People still appreciate a letter of thanks rather than a telephone call.

A letter, of course, is often sent to follow up a telephone call, providing a record of the points that were discussed and setting down the position that has now been reached.

Conversely, it is useful in many cases to write first and then follow up your letter by telephoning the person you have written to. For example, if you are a salesperson making an appointment with a prospective customer you can send him an introductory letter telling him something – just enough to whet his appetite – about your company and its products or services and how they can help him. In the closing paragraph of your letter you can put something like 'I will telephone you later this week to find out whether it would be convenient for me to come and see you next Thursday afternoon'. Of course letters like this should make your products or services sound interesting so the prospective customer will not discard your letter – and it goes without saying that a duplicated or printed letter of this kind would almost certainly be put straight into the wastepaper bin. Give your letters the personal touch.

If you are communicating with someone whose mother-tongue is not English and you feel there might be language difficulties, it is better to write a letter, or for speed send a Telex or telegram, rather than telephone, because the written word is generally easier to understand.

Taking incoming calls

It is important to give callers a good impression of your organization by the way their telephone calls are handled by the switchboard operator and by the people they speak to within the organization.

As well as having a pleasant, distinct voice, a switchboard operator should be tactful and patient, particularly when dealing with 'awkward customers'.

You can help your switchboard operator by making sure he or she has a note of your correct telephone extension, and your secretary's and assistant's extension numbers. Tell the switchboard operator the type of routine telephone calls to put through to your department. If you leave your telephone for any length of time, let the switchboard operator know where you can be reached. If the person a caller asks for is not available, let the caller know when the person is expected to be free and ask whether someone else can help them or if they would prefer to leave a message or to telephone again later. Write down all the telephone messages you take – the shortest pencil is better than the longest memory!

If you have been out of the office, or in a meeting, let the switchboard operator know when you return to your office and find out whether there have been any messages for you. Make sure you get written telephone messages, with the person's telephone number and extension. Ask your switchboard operator to encourage people to telephone you again, rather than to ask you to call them back. This will help to reduce the company's telephone bill. However, the switchboard should still take the names and telephone numbers of these callers, making a note that the caller will telephone again.

Always have paper and pen ready to write notes when you take a telephone call.

Telephone messages

Telephone messages can be recorded on pre-printed slips like this one, and should in any case include this sort of information, whether or not printed forms are used.

```
┌─────────────────────────────────────────┐
│                                           │
│  Time ..................                   │
│                                           │
│  Date ...............                      │
│                                           │
│  To ................. Dept .................│
│                                           │
│          TELEPHONE MESSAGE                │
│                                           │
│  Mr/Mrs/Miss/Ms ...........................│
│                                           │
│  of ........................ telephoned   │
│                                           │
│  about ...................................│
│                                           │
│  .........................................│
│                                           │
│  .........................................│
│                                           │
│  He/she will call again                   │
│                                           │
│  Please call him/her ........ Urgent ......│
│                                           │
│  Caller's phone No. .......... Extension ..│
│                                           │
│  Message taken by ........................│
│                                           │
└─────────────────────────────────────────┘
```

Not only the switchboard operator but also the person at the extension should answer the telephone as soon as possible, since telephone calls are expensive. The telephonist should be instructed to give the name of the organization so that if you are answering an extension you need only announce the name of your department or your own name. Then ask the caller how you can help them.

Telephone calls should not be transferred from one extension to another unless you are sure the person at the extension is available and can deal with the call.

Some telephone systems allow you to 'hold' an outside call, dial and speak to another extension inside your own organization and then come back to the outside call. Or you may be able to contact another department on an internal telephone system to make sure they can accept the call. If there is any doubt, it is best to offer to ring the caller back when you have the information they need.

Making outgoing calls

As with an incoming call, the people you speak to on the telephone will get an impression of your organization from the way you handle telephone conversations. Speak clearly and distinctly. If you have several points to discuss or the call is likely to be a 'difficult' one, it might be a good idea to jot down the main points of your proposed discussion on a piece of paper and have that in front of you as you speak. You can use it almost as an actor uses a script. Make sure any documents and files you might need to consult or quote from are within easy reach, so you do not have to leave the phone to fetch them. Always have paper and pen ready to write notes. Start by saying who you are and then go on to explain why you are telephoning. Try to keep your call as short as possible.

When telephoning inland remember that you may be able to take advantage of cheap, off-peak rates. If you are telephoning another country do not forget that there may be a time difference and try to make your call at an hour which will be convenient to both parties. If you are telephoning long distance and wish to speak to one person in particular it may be a good idea to make a Personal call, through the operator. Though there is a charge for this service, you will not start to pay for the actual call until the person you want comes on the line.

If you telephone someone and are informed by the switchboard that the person is already engaged in a telephone conversation or is out of the room, it is often cheaper to ring back later, rather than to hold on for him or her.

Golden rules of telephoning

* dial carefully (in the case of circular dials, rather than the press-button ones, you will also have to wait for the dial to return.)
* speak clearly and pleasantly
* answer the telephone quickly and say immediately who you are. Then go on to ask your caller how you can help him.
* Keep paper and pencil near the telephone so that you can make notes or take messages.
* If you are taking a telephone message for someone who is not available make a clear note of the caller's name and telephone number.
* Be brief. Don't get side-tracked. If you are a sales person trying to fix an appointment with a customer, for example, don't describe your product on the telephone – otherwise you will have done away with the need for the appointment you are trying to arrange.

The Telex

The Telex is a teleprinter – a means of instant written communication between two subscribers. Operated by the Post Office, the Telex also provides a cheaper method than the telephone of transmitting a message, whilst retaining the speed. Messages may be sent to and received by a subscriber even when his Telex is unattended, for example at night. This is particularly useful where a business needs to communicate with subscribers overseas, where there may be a difference between local times. Since Telex is a twenty-four hour service, it is also possible to send messages after office hours, so that the matter can be dealt with first thing in the morning.

Telex subscribers may also send and receive telegrams by Telex.

Sending messages by Telex

The Telex machine prints figures and capital letters only. When quoting figures it is often a good idea to type them out in words as well, to avoid misunderstanding. Fractions should be expressed 1/3 for ⅓, 3/4 for ¾. For a whole number and a fraction together, use a hyphen without spacing between the number and the fraction, thus 4-1/2 for 4½. For inverted commas use the apostrophe sign twice. When making a tape, corrections can be made before the Telex is sent out. If you are not using a tape and make an error, a quick way to correct it is to type the letter X five times after the erroneous word, leave a space and then type the word correctly. An alternative method is to type E space E space E and continue.

The Facsimile Machine (*Fax machine*)

Facsimile (popularly known as fax) is a method of sending documents containing text and graphical detail. Fax terminals look similar to photo-copiers except that they have a telephone number and ordinary exchange line connection to the public telephone system. The sending fax machine scans and converts the document into electrical signals which are subsequently transmitted over the telephone network to the receiving fax machine which reproduces an identical copy of the original document.

Sending and receiving documents by facsimile machine

Place the message on the document feed and dial the telephone number of the receiving fax machine. Normally the machines are programmed to receive calls automatically. If this is the case, after a few bursts of ringing tone, a high pitched tone follows and the sender proceeds by pressing the 'SEND' key on the machine. If the machine is set on manual reply, the recipient will press their 'RECEIVE' key which will bring the high pitched tone on to the line so that the sender can press the 'SEND' key, as before. When set on automatic, facsimile machines can receive documents without operator intervention.

International Telegrams

Though less common than they used to be, because of the development of Telex and teleprinters, telegrams still offer a quick reliable method of transmitting written information. Telegrams are charged by the word and so are expensive. Only the essential words should be included in the message, therefore, though it is important not to condense the message to such a degree as to make it ambiguous. The best way to draft a telegram is to write the message first in ordinary English and then to rephrase it, deleting all unnecessary words.

The hints on page 17, *Avoid circumlocution!* are even more important when drafting a telegram than they are when writing a letter. Instead of saying 'we are unable to be of assistance to you' say 'we cannot help you'. 'Telegraphic English', as it is known, is a way of expressing oneself in concise phrases which would be out of place in a letter, but which, so long as they are not ambiguous, are perfectly acceptable in a telegram. Don't forget that when calculating the cost of sending a telegram, punctuation and other signs are all treated as words so should be used only when necessary to avoid ambiguity and then written as words, STOP, COMMA. All figures should be expressed in words. Approved abbreviations, for example C/O, are counted as one word. Initial letters of organizations and businesses if written without stops in between the letters, e.g. NATO, BBC, are counted as one word.

In Britain any group of up to ten characters counts as one word, for the purposes of working out the costs of sending a telegram. Over ten characters count as two words or more. For example, REF/3/X has seven characters, so is charged as one word. METROPOLITAN has twelve characters, so is charged as two words. So where you can, use a short word − REMUNERATION is charged as two words but PAY is charged as one!

Telegrams can be sent by telephone or Telex or they may be handed in at a Post Office. In this case they should be typed or written in block letters on a standard telegram form.

You may take the precaution of confirming your telegram by letter.

Where an organization has a Telegraphic Address (see below) it will save you money if you use it. Add the organization's full name and address to your file copy of the telegram. Your name, address and telephone number should be recorded on the back of the telegram form, though they will not be telegraphed unless included in your message.

9 How to Dictate — The Great Dictator

There is an art to dictating. If you can learn this art you can help your typist produce better work and more of it.

You may choose to use a dictating machine — a very useful way of saving both your time and the typist's — or you can employ shorthand dictation. The method you use will depend on personal preference but if you have a strong foreign accent, or a bad stammer, you would be well advised not to use a machine.

Whichever method you use you should always give the typist as much work as possible early in the day. It's not unusual for a typist to sit with no work all morning and then to be asked to work late to type a complicated report.

If you are using a dictating machine speak directly into it, try to keep the machine roughly the same distance away from you and in the same position all the time so that the typist will not have to adjust the volume too frequently. Speak in your normal voice at a normal speed. Try to chose a quiet place to dictate — your machine will pick up the noises around you, like telephones ringing and people arguing in the office next door.

Whether you are dictating into a machine or to someone taking shorthand, treat your typist as a person who wants to present the best work possible. Start by thanking the typist for the work he or she did last time for you. Find out his or her name and use it. Be human. Go easy though on the bonhomie. No typist with a lot of work to get through wants to listen to a series of anecdotes and the jokes heard in the pub last night. Whilst dictating resist the temptation to march up and down the room, and don't smoke or suck peppermints.

If you are using shorthand dictation, don't waste your typist's time. Sort out your papers, check information and make your telephone calls before calling the typist in. Keep correspondence clipped together in the order you are going to answer it, or number the letters for easy reference. Give these letters to the typist so that he or she can check addresses and other details.

Before the typist can start typing he or she must be told exactly what kind of work you are planning — a letter, a report, a memorandum and so on, and given such additional information as how long the piece of typing is likely to be, what sort of paper you want used, what typeface you want if your typist is using a golf-ball typewriter, how many copies you want, and whether you want carbons or photocopies, any parti-cular style the typist should use — or do you always use the 'house style', any unusual setting for line lengths or whether single or double line spacing should be used. If the typing is likely to run to more than one page tell the typist if there are any special points that should be borne in mind with the layout of the continuation sheets. If you are using a machine rather than shorthand dictation you should make doubly sure that all your instructions are very clear as the typist will not be able to ask you to clarify any points he or she does not understand. If you are dic-tating face to face ask the person taking the shorthand notes whether they have understood the instructions and give them the opportunity to ask questions.

Just because you know Mr Browne in the Buying Department spells his name with a final 'e' please do not assume that every typist knows. Conversely typists are not duffers and if you write to Mr Browne every day, don't insult your typist by spelling out his name every single time. Iron out problems before they happen by spelling out any difficult words or technical terms or by writing them down for the typist. Always indicate if a word should be underlined or typed in capital letters. When using a dictating machine it is particularly important to tell the typist that the work is *going* to be in capitals rather than saying, 'Oh, by the way, you should have typed that in upper case'. You'll only infuriate the typist — and quite rightly — and cause him or her to produce poor copy. If your shorthand typist does not hear a word and asks you to repeat it, do so clearly, do not shout. Decide in advance whether you are going to dictate all punctuation marks and then stick to your decisions. Nothing is more irritating for the typist than inconsistency on the part of the person dictating. And if you employ intelligent staff please remember that it is insulting to a typist if you dictate 'new paragraph, capital letter'. The capital letter should be obvious.

If you do employ intelligent staff you might recognise it once in a while by leaving the wording of some straightforward letters to the typist. Just make sure you give him or her all the information needed to compose the letter.

Make full use of a standard form letter book to cut down routine dictation (see page 132).

There may be times when you will want something typed from a draft in longhand. Obviously the neater your writing and the better your spelling the more likely you are to get a well-typed document back. If your writing is really appalling you should certainly consider typing that document yourself. If you are writing out figures use lined paper and lay the figures out in the way you wish the typed document to look. Don't alter figures or words by writing the correct words over those previously inserted — cross the word through and make the alteration neatly. Don't scrawl all over your draft with sketches of your boss, balloons, asterisks and arrows. If you are making corrections use the correct proof readers' marks if possible.

When the typed documents are given to you, check them carefully. Not only is it impolite to send out a letter with typing errors, it also makes your letters more difficult to read. Every time a reader comes across a typing mistake he has to pause, and this pause, however brief, will distract him and make it less easy for him to follow your thoughts. If the typist has made mistakes, indicate the alterations — preferably on the carbon copy or on a separate piece of paper or else lightly in pencil on the original top copy — and return the work for correction. Again, if you can use the standard proof-reading correction symbols do so. Should you wish to write any notes to the typist that you do not want typed, preface them with the word typist, or better still, with the typist's name, and put a ring round them.

Don't stand over the typist while he or she is completing an urgent piece of typing or making a complicated alteration which needs concentration.

Finally, it shouldn't be necessary to remind you that thanks and a few words of praise for a job well done will work wonders in terms of goodwill.

And a word to the typist ...

Let's hope the people who dictate to you follow the advice in the section above, and so help to make your work easier and pleasurable. If you have the sort of boss who dictates through clenched teeth and then rushes in at two-minute intervals to see if you have finished the ten urgent letters you were given less than ten minutes ago, perhaps you can leave this book open for them to read.

However considerate your boss, the best maxim is to disbelieve everything he or she says. If he writes to "Dear Mrs Metcalf" check previous correspondence to make sure he does not usually write "Dear Sue". If he refers to "Your letter of 9th June" check the date, or that when the letter says "I will come back to you on Wednesday 9th" the 9th really is a Wednesday.

When taking shorthand pay attention to what is being said and follow the sense of the letter, It's all too easy to take everything down on 'automatic pilot' and then to find you cannot read anything between 'Dear Sir' and 'Yours faithfully'.